To Simon
with thanks

Ralph Lewis

Designed and Published by E-Mediate Books Ltd.
April 2014

ISBN: 978-0-9569989-4-1

Front cover: *"Thoughts"*,
a painting by Ahrabella Heabe Lewis
© Ahrabella Heabe Lewis (www.ahrabellaheabelewis.co.uk).

Developing Inner Leadership:

A Pathway to Wholeness

Ralph Lewis

"*Developing Inner Leadership* is a practical handbook and resource for connecting and aligning with our deeper selves.

The reflective inquiries and numerous exercises take us on a gentle stroll and journey into the wholeness and knowing that already lay at the very center of our innermost being. There, we are able to reclaim our core values, dreams, and gifts, returning afterward to the world of work and family with integrity, joy, and the generosity of spirit... Do yourself and world a favor – take the journey!"

George San Facon,
A Conscious Person's Guide to the Workplace.

"*Developing Inner Leadership* is a remarkably wise and wonderful book. In the tradition of Peter Drucker and Robert Greenleaf, Ralph Lewis knows how to ask powerful questions of us while offering realistic and useful advice on how to better serve and lead others.

The exercises and diagrams included in this book provide a powerful pathway toward personal leadership development. Grounded in personal story and practices and its impact in leading organisational change, *Developing Inner Leadership* is vital reading."

Larry C Spears,
author/editor,
Insights on Leadership
President,
The Spears Center for Servant-Leadership, Indianapolis, Indiana.
Servant-Leadership Scholar,
Gonzaga University, Spokane, Washington.

With *Inner Leadership* Ralph Lewis illustrates, by illuminating and powerful processes, a way through the tangle of reaction we often fall victim to – on our way to the mastery of choice in action.

He does this with wit and charm revealing a path to a contagious state of grace in honouring the authenticity of our own peace. The leader in ourselves becomes a magnet for others, to not only follow, but to gain inspiration from. In this way we reflect what inspires us and, in turn, may find this inspiring too.

This book provides a clear message for all seeking greater freedom of choice within themselves when faced with decisions regarding business and life. If unexamined our views only mirror our personal experiences through the limited scope of loss and gain and not through the light of total clarity and possibility.

By combining a wide cultural spectrum of wisdom and ideas he elegantly weaves a path to this light taking into consideration our innate human frailty as well as our potential greatness. His work is an invaluable tool for all those aspiring to deliver conscious business ethics in these challenging times.

Safaya Salter,
Inspirational Life Coach and Energy Therapist.

Meet the author

Ralph Lewis is a Leadership Development consultant with a career that has included engineering, systems analysis and university lecturing. He has worked in the computing, pharmaceutical, finance, and public sectors and geographically in Europe, USA, Asia and Africa and published several books and many articles. He is also a co-founder of the UK Centre for Servant-Leadership.

He based *Developing Inner Leadership* on his experience with thousands of leaders to help them to develop a more encompassing view of themselves and of their lives rather than focusing on one aspect to the detriment of the others. By seeing life in its entirety it can become easier for them, and for others, to lead the lives they wish for and deserve.

Acknowledgements

I'd like to thank everyone who I've had long and short discussions with over the years on leadership, life, Jung and work – my colleagues and the many participants who have been so great to work with.

Especially thanks go to Lynda McGill for her superb editing beyond the call of duty and to my wonderful publisher Hazel Wood.

Also a great many thanks to Ahrabella Hebe Lewis for permission to use her painting for the cover – she is an inspiration.

Ralph Lewis

Contents

Exercises

Diagrams

Foreword

I have frequently seen people become neurotic when they content themselves with inadequate or wrong answers to the questions of life. They seek position, marriage, reputation, outward success or money, and remain unhappy and neurotic even when they have attained what they were seeking. Such people are usually contained within too narrow a spiritual horizon. Their life has not sufficient content, sufficient meaning; if they are enabled to develop into more spacious personalities the neurosis generally disappears

Carl Jung

In the many workshops and development programmes I have run with thousands of participants I have seen many people put a focus on one part of their lives to the exclusion of the rest of their world. They blame either other people or the environment or themselves in that they feel worthless or powerless. And then they try to fix things by therapy or switching jobs or changing their relationships or learning new skills.

But we need to consider everything that affects us when we hope to change for the better. Our actions come from a combination of our personalities, the people around us, our abilities and what's going on in the world. If we do not look at all these aspects then our actions will not be successful. This is why Inner Leadership is so important; it enables each of us to be clear about what we need to do in all the areas of our lives to be successful overall.

Inner Leadership is an approach to looking at these areas through a combination of exercises and processes to support and encourage each of us in our own unique journey.

Inner Leadership is about being true to yourself and doing what you need to do because it is right for you. It doesn't matter to the Inner Leader whether they have followers or not – their own inner vision is what counts for them.

It is about honouring and respecting yourself without the arrogance of certainty. And if the Inner Leader truly honours and values him or herself, then they will honour and value others as well.

At the core of all of us – acknowledged or not – is a deep caring for and connection with all life. There are many obstacles, external, but more often than not internal to reaching this inner base of caring, security and joy. Not the least is fear and following on from that the confusion that results from all the stuff we take on board from others that doesn't belong to us.

Our task is to understand and release the barriers that have blocked us, through no fault of our own, from being in touch with this source. Once we have done this, like clearing the clouds that stop the sun from reaching us, we can express our joy and caring for the benefit of others.

Inner Leadership is for those who want to undertake this journey to their source and to emerge back into the world as a true Inner Leader – one who cares and is strong enough to do what is right! This may or may not be a difficult or easy journey – that depends on what we need to let go of – but the final destination is one we will all arrive at – peace and joy and a sense of who we really are.

Chapter 1:

Introduction:
How to Discover Your Inner Leader

The highest reward for man's toil is not
what he gets for it but what he becomes by it.
John Ruskin

If you do not go within, you go without
Neale Donald Walsh

How to Discover Your Inner Leader

For many of us our schooling or work is about success "out there" – to be measured by exam passes, money or by promotion. But also for most of us what really counts are our own feelings of success. What happens out there is important but we need to be at peace with ourselves and to live a life that feels meaningful and worthwhile.

To do this we need to realise that school is over! We are our own authority and it's the marks that we give ourselves that count most. Of course it is important to be aware of others and their views but in the end we need to live the lives and serve the purposes that we were born for.

This means developing our own sense of who we are and becoming the best we can be – for ourselves. And this is about the practical wisdom of life – not theory without practice. To do this we need to explore our inner world and what makes us truly unique.

No-one else can tell us that; they can help – but we need to listen to ourselves. And paradoxically we can do that best by listening and talking to others.

So specifically our Inner Leadership goals or intentions are to:

Let go of our fears and to live our lives fully as ourselves.

To love being with others regardless of who they are.

To wake up every morning with a zest for whatever will happen that day.

We can do this best by:

Celebrating and being grateful for whatever happens.

Letting go of trying to figure things out.

Being open to receiving.

Celebrating the uniqueness of each person, including ourselves.

It's as simple as that but of course getting there might or might not be so easy.

The Pathway to Inner Leadership

This is not really a journey or pathway in the sense of a set of steps to be followed to get to a final destination. The route needs to be created by you as you work through the key areas of your life. The suggestion is that you start with looking at your life as a whole via Chapter Two and answer the Vital Questions.

From there identify which area you feel is most important to you and start with that; complete the other areas and then go to the final section Chapter Seven (Inner Leadership and Play).

So, after the Vital Questions and Living on Purpose, what is a key area for you? It is important to recognise that wherever we start we will need to revisit it after going through the other areas as it will be affected by them.

Someone looking for a career change might identify their skills, their values and the type of work and organisation that would be ideal for them as a start. However, because of the need to look at life as a whole the demands of their family might be more important than their career and, therefore, they would need to modify their way forward. For example many people hold back on job and location changes because it would mean disrupting their children's education.

A guide to the key areas follows. This is to give you a sense of what the key areas are and how they fit together before plunging into each area in depth.

Chapter 2. Inner Leadership: Living Life as a Whole

The beginning of any endeavour is vital. Even though the Inner Leader may not know his or her final destination or be clear about their purpose they need to prepare and set a direction for their initial steps. We will use a variety of exercises, visualisations and other work to help the Inner Leader begin to answer questions such as these.

What does Inner Leadership mean for me?

What is the balance of my head and my heart?

What are my answers to the vital questions? – My values, strengths and my companions?

How can I discover my purpose and then live it?

How can I change easily and joyfully?

Chapter 3. Telling My Story

All of us have a unique story which is the way we view our lives. Sometimes the story may be very helpful but more often than not there will be elements which we need to let go of and we then need to rewrite our story to progress on our inner journey.

What has been my unique journey?

What roles and characters have I played?

What parts of the story still work for me and what do I need to let go of?

How can I uncreate my limiting beliefs?

Who are my inner heroes?

Chapter 4. Being Your Best

So much focus is often on the negative – what we need to do to improve, be better etc. and we often take for granted all those areas that we are good at and tell ourselves, "well anyone can do that!", when of course they can't! Focusing on what we are good at and building on this gives us confidence and strength and the potential to be brilliant at our own unique contribution.

When I am at my best I am like...

What are my unique strengths and talents?

How can I develop and use my strengths?

What's the right work and organisation for me?

Developing a Practice

A practice is a daily set of disciplines (discipline originally means learning not painful processes!). By developing a practice along with other companions we can make our journey both fun and meaningful. So the key question is:

What do I need to do daily for my own growth, peace and joy?

Shadow Work

There is the other side to being our best of course – the "Shadow". The Shadow is only that which has not yet been brought into the light – and as Robert Johnson, a brilliant Jungian analyst, has said: "Shadow work contains Inner Gold. By shining a light on those parts of ourselves that contain our deepest fears or anger we can transform them into our service."

What is my shadow? The inner barriers I have? My Inner critic?

How can I turn this to gold?

What inner work do I need to do?

Chapter 5. Companions

Jung once said: "It's never a question of what; it's always a question of who!" Other people are the arena for our growth and both trials and joys. We need to treat others as ourselves with respect and care, but that doesn't mean staying in relations that demean us.

Knowing what is needed from relationships will help the Inner Leader be with those who support and lighten their load.

What do I need from others? Significance, Control and Love?

Who are my companions?

Who lightens my spirits?

And how do I attract those I love being with?

Discovering the Masculine and Feminine in each of us

Jung talked of men containing an inner feminine and women containing an inner masculinity. These are complementary energies that need to be balanced and used positively for the Inner Leader to be complete.

What do I need from my "other" side?

What does love mean for me?

What are my blockages to receiving and sharing love?

How do I work with the masculine and feminine sides of myself?

Chapter 6. Leading Organisations

We all live and work in organisations. The simplest definition is a group of people with a common goal. So a family is an organisation. However, we all have preferences for what type of organisation we like to be in – whether at work or socially. So we need to understand what works for us.

What type of organisation is best for me?

What values must it have for me to be happy?

How can I lead at my best in organisations?

What teams do I enjoy being part of?

Chapter 7. Inner Leadership and Play

We cannot isolate parts of ourselves from other parts – all is an interconnected whole. This wholeness is our Self – the Holy Grail of our journey. And key to reaching this is play, fun and artistry – our own creativity in whatever way we express it!

What is my inner source? My inner artist?

What do I love playing at – and with whom?

How can I be guided by my wiser self?

How can I be truly happy?

How can I release my fears, hopes and judgements so I can be whole?

Chapter 8. The Selfdom Model

The Selfdom Model is a framework for looking at all the aspects of ourselves and all the interconnections we have in our inner world. Through this we can build a strong inner sanctuary for ourselves to guide us in our journey.

How can I discover my Inner Leader and recover my own power?
How can I develop my own voice?

Inner Work

Inner work needs to be done gently and patiently, allowing understanding to emerge – as Jung said, allowing stuff to cook slowly! We can divide this work into three stages:

1. **Personal Preparation** – reviewing history and development areas through developing calm and inner peace through reflection and becoming aware of your real needs (not wants). Then allowing yourself to let go of past limiting beliefs and enhancing your awareness.

2. **Building your own Practice Toolbox** – looking at tools and processes that will develop inner strengths through ways you most resonate with.

3. **Daily Practice** aimed at being authentic and developing flexibility of thought and action.

"Soft Thinking"

"Soft Thinking" is about allowing our unconscious which is often represented by an elephant (simply because it is so large and powerful) to absorb and react rather than just relying on our conscious mind (the rider of the elephant!)

Picture yourself riding the elephant and commanding it to go in the direction you want it to go. It's pretty obvious you can only suggest directions for the elephant, the real power lies with the elephant. And, as we shall see, the elephant mind responds more to images and metaphors than straight forward logic and analysis. In other words you have to be kind to it and to yourself as the "elephant".

This image of the rider and elephant is a good one to keep in mind in any change and applies equally to other people as well and explains why although our rational mind may decide to do something positive such as eating healthily the "elephant" continues with its old habits.

Chapter 2

Inner Leadership:
Living Life as a Whole

"I have looked at some training programs for leaders, and I am discouraged by how often they focus on the development of skills to manipulate the external world rather than the skills necessary to go within and make the spiritual journey. I find that discouraging because it feeds a dangerous syndrome among leaders who already tend to deny their inner world."

Parker Palmer

The mastery of the art of leadership comes with the mastery of the self.

J Kouzes

The aim of this chapter is to help you to see the key areas of your life and how they connect with each other.

The examination of each of these aspects may take some time, however it is critical to start with a good understanding of what your whole life context really is. From this base you can then start to use Inner Leadership techniques to help you to integrate these areas into a positive whole which will make successful change far more likely. So let's start with looking at Inner Leadership.

A. What is Inner Leadership?

The word "leader" is an Anglo-Saxon term which suggests a guide – someone who goes ahead to show the way. If you are leading the way then you set the direction, the ways of travelling, the "rules", especially of course if the territory is new and unknown. And the inner aspect of leadership comes from trusting your own intuition and values.

So who can teach you to be a leader? The short answer is: no-one! You can *learn* from others of course, from their experience and wisdom, but your journey will be special to you.

Inner Leadership is about this journey, about tapping into your own inner wisdom, self-knowledge and awareness – and leading yourself to your own unique destination: to fulfil your potential whatever that might be. It requires wisdom – the ability to move out from your conditioning and assumptions and to think through the consequences of your actions. So let's look at your views on leadership.

Exercise 1: World Leader

Imagine you have had a phone call from the Secretary General of the United Nations. All the countries of the world have agreed that they are going to elect a world government. They need someone to lead the world. So they are asking you for your advice. They also have, of course, a magic DNA machine so if you decided that someone from history (a real person) was the best candidate they could get that person for you. Who would be your choice and why?

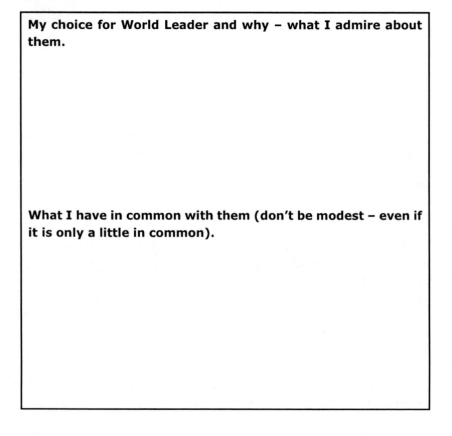

My choice for World Leader and why – what I admire about them.

What I have in common with them (don't be modest – even if it is only a little in common).

Exercise 2: So thinking about leaders you have known:

Who in your life do you admire as a leader and why? What did they do, what characteristics did they show?

And the reverse: who were the worst leaders you have known? And again why?

Exercise 3: Putting the above positives and the World Leader exercise together what characteristics would you like to have as a leader yourself?

Characteristics:

B. Head and Heart

Another way to think about leadership is to see it as a combination of getting work done and motivating people. The two essential attributes for these aspects are clarity (seeing what needs to be done, planning, problem-solving etc.) and empathy – understanding and relating to people. Or to put it more simply combining head and heart.

The Gallup survey of effective leaders found that one key trait they shared was the ability to recognise individual differences and make the most of this. In Inner Leadership you also need to use your heart to recognise individuality and your head to set the way forward for the people you are with.

This also applies to leading yourself. You need to be aligned with your deepest feelings and needs and take well considered appropriate actions that serve you and others. The head-heart balance is vital for true leadership.

Exercise 4: My Head-Heart Balance

For a different take on your Head-Heart balance look at a superb talk on

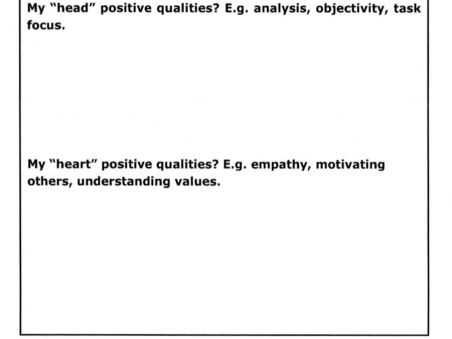

My "head" positive qualities? E.g. analysis, objectivity, task focus.

My "heart" positive qualities? E.g. empathy, motivating others, understanding values.

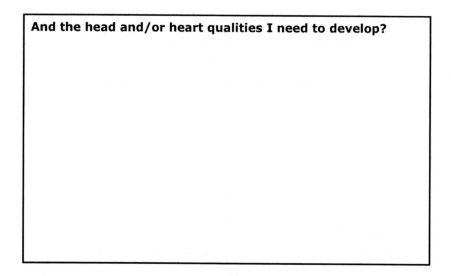

And the head and/or heart qualities I need to develop?

TED by Itay Talgam: *Lead like the great conductors.*

You can find it at:

www.ted.com/talks/lang/en/itay_talgam_lead_like_the_great_conductors.html

You can see in the different head-heart leadership styles between Carlos Klieber and Ricardo Mutti for example.

C. The Vital Questions

We can use the Head-Heart distinction to look at different parts of our world and further divide this into what's out there in the world (the environment and other people) and what's in us – our personalities, and skills. These are the key factors that interact with each other and make up our view of the world and ourselves.

It is also very important that we do not confuse these areas.

For example some people's view of themselves could be based solely on others' views of them or their talents or their worldly success without taking into account their own unique personality.

The Vital Questions are the starting point for our Inner Leadership search and set the groundwork for all to come. The diagram on the next page represents the External-Internal and Head-Heart aspects of ourselves.

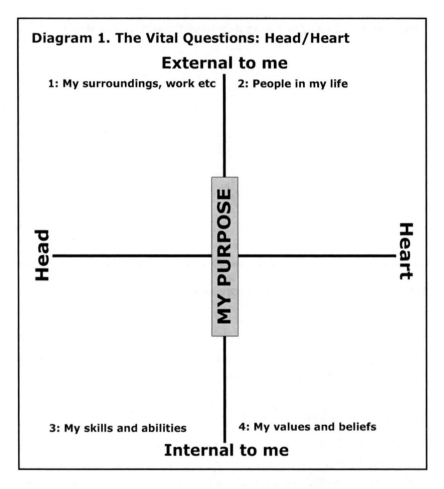

Diagram 1. The Vital Questions: Head/Heart

External to me

1: My surroundings, work etc

2: People in my life

Head

MY PURPOSE

Heart

3: My skills and abilities

4: My values and beliefs

Internal to me

Quadrant 1 is about your external world – both physically and also economically, where you live, work, the organisation you are in, the money you earn. We need environments that offer us joy and growth rather than draining and exhausting us.

Quadrant 2 is the External Heart aspect of our world. It is the people in our life and how we interact with them and them with us. Hopefully we treat others as if they too have feelings and connect with them on a human level. Some people cannot do this unfortunately!

Quadrant 3 is about what is the more objective side of our world– what we can or can't do. It is objective because there are standards of performance we can be measured against. For example how good are we at, say, using spreadsheets or baking cakes? What are your skills?

And **quadrant 4,** Internal Heart is the hardest of all to define. It's what makes you the unique individual you are; your values and your unique experience. And as it's the area that is hardest to access it tends to be the area that is most neglected in our Western educational system. We are not taught how to deal with our feelings, for example.

All quadrants are important, but the Inner Heart quadrant – where we discover the essence of the true self – is the area which most concerns Inner Leadership.

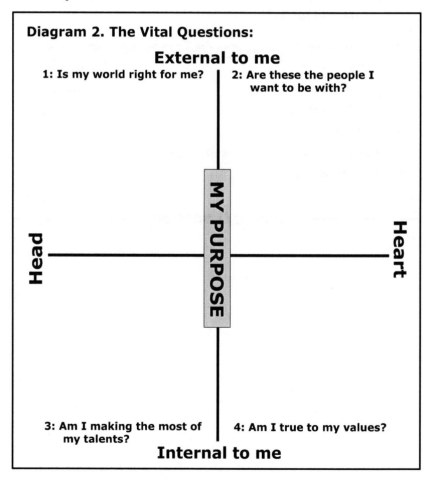

Diagram 2. The Vital Questions:

External to me

1: Is my world right for me?

2: Are these the people I want to be with?

Head

MY PURPOSE

Heart

3: Am I making the most of my talents?

4: Am I true to my values?

Internal to me

Developing Inner Leadership

How we treat others is a reflection of ourselves. What we do in the world, how we live, how we develop our talents – all are essential. The vital questions that relate to these areas help us to form our personal strategy for our life.

Complete these questions for yourself and keep coming back to them. Focus especially on the people side – this tends to be an area we don't pay as much attention to in Anglo-Saxon societies as in other countries. Keep coming back to this. What's working for you in each area? What needs fixing?

Exercise 5: The Vital Questions – Analysis

1. Is my world right for me?

How satisfied am I with my physical surroundings, home, and location?   (Marks out of 10)

My work and my organisation   (Marks out of 10)

What do I like about it?

What do I dislike?

What opportunities or problems are there?

What needs to change?

```
──────────────── Home/Location ────────────────
┌─────────────────────────────────────────────┐
│                                               │
│                                               │
│                                               │
│                                               │
│                                               │
└─────────────────────────────────────────────┘
```

Work/Organisation

2. Significant Others:

What are the relationships like with the significant others in my life
(at home, socially and at work?)

How satisfied am I with them?   (Marks out of 10)

Are they the people I would choose to be with?

What's right about these relationships?

What needs to improve?

Home/Social relationships

29

Work relationships

3. What are my strengths and talents?

Am I clear about what they are or could be?

Am I able to use them fully?   (Marks out of 10)

What do I need to develop?

What needs to change for me to use my strengths fully?

My strengths and talents

Am I able to apply them at work or elsewhere?

4. My values – am I clear about what they are?

Do I know what I love doing?

What I don't want to do?

Can I be myself fully? (Marks out of 10)

What needs to change?

My values, likes and dislikes?

What needs to change to allow me to be fully me?

Having looked at the key areas which would you say posed the greatest challenge to you and what is the effect of them on your life?

And, by the way, challenges are essential; if there was no friction we couldn't walk.

We have got on to slippery ice where there is no friction and so in a certain sense the conditions are ideal, but also, just because of that, we are unable to walk. We want to walk: so we need friction. Back to the rough ground!
Ludwig Wittgenstein,

Exercise 6: Life's Challenges

My challenges

The effects of these challenges on my life?

Exercise 7: What would you like to happen?

Imagine that you could solve these challenges overnight by the aid of a magic wand.

If you used it on these challenges what would happen?

What would be the plus side?

What would be the possible downside?

How would this change you?

Exercise 8: My Dreams / Ideal Day

Behind every great achievement is a dreamer of great dreams. Much more than a dreamer is needed to bring it to reality; but the dream must be there first.

Robert Greenleaf

Let's translate what you would like to happen into a more systematic analysis by using the vital question areas again. Imagine it's a perfect day. You wake up full of joy. Your heart is singing and there is a spring in your step. You are in the perfect place with those you most want to be with and doing the work you love. Go through the day seeing, feeling, and imagining the ideal day for you.

Describe the day below then answer the questions in Diagram 3.

```
┌──────────────── My ideal day ────────────────┐
│                                               │
│                                               │
│                                               │
│                                               │
│                                               │
│                                               │
│                                               │
│                                               │
└───────────────────────────────────────────────┘
```

In order to make progress towards your dreams you need to do some more work. Let's start with your purpose.

D. Living on Purpose

The aim of life is to live, and to live means to be aware, joyously, drunkenly, serenely, divinely aware.

Henry Miller

And those who were dancing were thought insane by those who could not hear the music.

Nietzsche

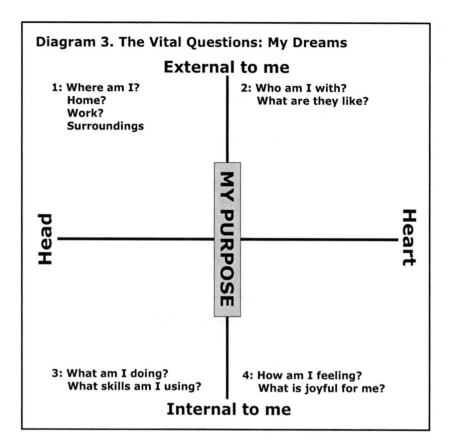

Diagram 3. The Vital Questions: My Dreams

External to me

1: Where am I?
Home?
Work?
Surroundings

2: Who am I with?
What are they like?

MY PURPOSE

Head

Heart

3: What am I doing?
What skills am I using?

4: How am I feeling?
What is joyful for me?

Internal to me

All this analysis! All this thinking! And you wanted a quiet life! But more work (or play) to come. Dreams do need to be translated into the world of action. So let's start with purpose.

Robert Scheinfeld, author of *Busting Loose from the Business Game,* has some great thoughts on this. Essentially whether we are aware of it or not we are living the purpose we are meant to be living and it's probably best not to waste too much time getting hung up on what that should or should not be.

As long as we are moving in a direction that feels right for us and for those around us – and we are letting go of the burdens of our lives and freeing ourselves from being dragged down by others – that's probably good enough. And life purpose can be as simple and profound as having fun! (See Henry Miller above) or as Joseph Campbell said: *"Follow Your Bliss"*

However, if you want to have a go at finding your "purpose" try the following.

Exercise 9: My "Purpose"

What do I love doing? What skills, talents am I using? And what is the positive impact on those around me?

┌───────────── **I love doing:** ─────────────┐
│   │
│   │
│   │
│   │
│   │
│   │
└──┘

┌──────── **I am using my talents for:** ────────┐
│   │
│   │
│   │
│   │
│   │
└──┘

┌────────── **And the impact on others:** ──────────┐
│   │
│   │
│   │
│   │
│   │
└──┘

Therefore, my purpose is:

To use my talents of:

_____

When doing:

_____

So that people :

_____

Service

> _In serving others we become free._
> **Inscribed on King Arthur's Round Table**

> _I believe that service – whether it is serving the community or your family or the people you love or whatever – is fundamental to what life is about._
> **Anita Roddick**

Your purpose may well involve service to others. So much research has shown that we are truly happy only when we lose sight of our own needs and are helping others. (Note this does not mean being a doormat or doing things unwillingly!) There is a whole philosophy around this – Servant-Leadership developed by Robert Greenleaf which Inner Leaders may find inspiring.

> _The servant-leader is servant first. It begins with the natural feeling that one wants to serve, to serve first. Then conscious choice brings one to aspire to lead. The difference manifests itself in the care taken by the servant-first to make sure that other people's highest priorities are being served. The best test, and difficult to administer, is: Do those served grow as persons? Do they, while being served, become healthier, wiser, freer, more autonomous, more likely themselves to become servants? And what is the effect on the least privileged in society; will they benefit or, at least, not be further deprived?_
> **Robert Greenleaf**

Becoming Clearer

As you begin to be clearer about your world and what's right for you the next stage is to make certain that you are moving in the direction you want to go. It is helpful to focus on the following questions in Exercise 10 and keep coming back to them – both in terms of planning what you will be doing and then reviewing what worked or what didn't work. You may become clearer about what things you do because you haven't questioned them before; or because you realise other people want you to do them rather than it's what YOU really want to do!

This is not about selfishness – putting a smile on someone's face is about benefiting them and you – but the point is to do these activities whole-heartedly.

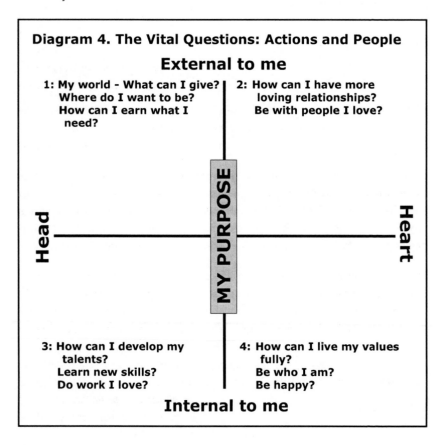

Diagram 4. The Vital Questions: Actions and People

External to me

1: My world - What can I give? Where do I want to be? How can I earn what I need?

2: How can I have more loving relationships? Be with people I love?

Head

MY PURPOSE

Heart

3: How can I develop my talents? Learn new skills? Do work I love?

4: How can I live my values fully? Be who I am? Be happy?

Internal to me

Exercise 10: Activity and People Planning

Take your dream from Exercise 8 and your purpose from Exercise 9 and, with these in mind, what do you need to do to realise them? What do you need to change? What about your Leadership qualities, Head and Heart? How will they help you? What needs to happen in each of the arenas to help you move in the direction you want to go? Use Diagram 4 to help to explore your answers.

It's a good idea to focus on time for your family, friends, community and certainly "you" time! If you want to love your neighbour as yourself it's a good idea to starting by loving yourself more!

Be specific in each of the areas – what is it you really would like to have happen? The guidelines from the Sedona Method (www.Sedonamethod.com) can be helpful.

Phrase goals/intentions in the "now" not the future as it will always be out of reach.

Be positive – put in what outcome you would like to have, not what you don't want

Make it real and realistic to you but allow for surprises (of a good sort). Use the phrase "I allow myself to." Never use the word "want" as it demonstrates a lack of. For example: From now on I allow myself to listen fully to people.

Goals / Intentions:

Arena 1 – My world

Arena 2 – Relationships

Arena 3 – My talents

Arena 4 – My values and feelings

And out of all this – your top four priorities

My top priorities

1:

2:

3:

4:

All this should help you to decide **each day** what is important to you. The following questions will help:

For every activity ask: Does this support who I choose to be?
Do I choose to do this?

For every relationship ask: Do they support who I choose to be?
And what I choose to do and have?

If activities or people sap your energy see if you can stop the activity or find someone else to be with.

Try experimenting – having Activity Days where you change one of your usual habits and see whether this is helpful to your purpose. And likewise having People Days where maybe you listen more or go out of your way to make friends or help someone else. Reflect and review – again what works, what doesn't.

Writing down a daily Gratitude list of things you are grateful for, no matter how small, helps to energise you and move you in a positive direction.

E. Change

The paradox of change – the more we want or try to change the more we get in the way; the more we accept the present the easier it is to change.

Change happens naturally and easily. For example our individual beliefs have changed since we were children. Everything changes and flows in time – like rivers going to the sea. We can try to stop change by resisting it, like building a dam across a river – but sooner or later change will happen.

Having said that, sometimes resistance to change acts as a very positive sign. It may suggest that there are genuine fears or doubts we need to look at more deeply before moving on. Though there is a saying that *"What you resist persists!"* So be aware that long-held fears or doubts can exert negative power and hold you back from change.

How change happens is often as important as what the change is. Those of you with teenagers will know that telling or ordering them to do something often will not work. They wish to be treated as the emerging adults they are and be asked to do things not told. This is a lesson that many leaders could do with understanding when they enforce change on their employees or followers.

Below is a process for working with issues of change. (This is modified from a superb process by Chris Payne which I recommend highly – the Complete Acceptance Process). As always, modify it to suit yourself and it can be helpful to work with someone else.

Change Process

Each step involves scoring yourself out of ten for that particular aspect. So Step 1 Relaxing in the Now would be scoring yourself out of ten for how present and relaxed you are NOW! If the score is low, say 4, you say to yourself *"Can I let this increase?"* and allow it to get as high as it can.

1. **Relax in the Now** – focus on the present

2. **Commit to Goals** – how committed out of 10 are you to that goal? This is

a very useful way of testing whether you really want that goal or it is there because it is a "Should". If you are trying to get your commitment to increase but it will not get higher then you need to re-examine why you are setting yourself that goal.

3. Honour and accept fully any resistance e.g. what are the advantages of not changing? With all change there is a cost – time, energy, emotional wear and tear etc. Resistance to changing, even if we think we would like the new state, is a normal reaction.

Often there are advantages to not changing even if we do not know what they are. The process here is the same as above; accept the resistance as fully as you can as shown by scoring your acceptance out of 10.

If you can accept the resistance fully it often disappears because you have acknowledged to yourself the valid downsides of the change you are proposing. If it persists then it is time for some deep thinking about the goal.

4. Limiting Beliefs – what stops you achieving these goals? These are your thoughts about the situation and can be many and varied. E.g. I'm lazy; the economic climate is too difficult.

In Chapter 3 there is a section on dealing with limiting beliefs which you can use to deal with these. Byron Katie has some superb questions for looking at these as well which you can download from her website. E.g. Is it true? Is it absolutely true?

5. Empowering Resources – what do you have (Inner and Outer resources)? For example have you dealt successfully with changes like this in your past?

Are there other people who can support you?

Again commit to using your resources fully (out of 10 again)

6. What's the next step? Commit fully to doing this

Exercise 11. Applying the Change Process to my Goals

Take one of your priority goals and work your way through Diagram 5. The Change Process which is on the next two pages.

Diagram 5. The Change Process

Relax in the Now

Let Go worry/fear anger just for Now

Clearing mental or emotional clutter

Appreciation of the present.

Relaxed out of 10?

Priority:

First step:

Next:

Next:

Goal:

Priority:

First step:

Next:

Next:

Goal:

Allow/Choose/Aims/ Goals

Clarity/Commitment

Be, do, have

Being true to yourself check with head and heart

Commitment out of 10?

Resistance/Limiting Factors

Honour and accept

Advantages of not changing?

Fear of: success/failure /consequences

Acceptance of valid reasons out of 10

Priority:

First step:

Next:

Next:

Goal:

The Change Process. Diagram 5

Priority:
_____

First step:
_____

Next:
_____

Next:
_____

Goal:
_____

Empowering Resources

Celebrating/Energising /Joy and Power/ Confidence

Inner Resources (and Outer)

Past History

Role Models

Maximising resources out of 10

Actions

?

Commitment out of 10?

Priority:
_____

First step:
_____

Next:
_____

Next:
_____

Goal:
_____

Allow for surprises and smile!

In other words, having done all this work and taken the first step, expect the best to happen.

F. Summing Up

Exercise 12: Summing Up.

Having done all this work it can be very helpful to have it all on one piece of paper in front of you so you can see interconnections and how different parts of your world need to be integrated. So summarise (and keep updating) the conclusions, issues, goals, actions etc. you have committed to in each of the areas of the vital questions.

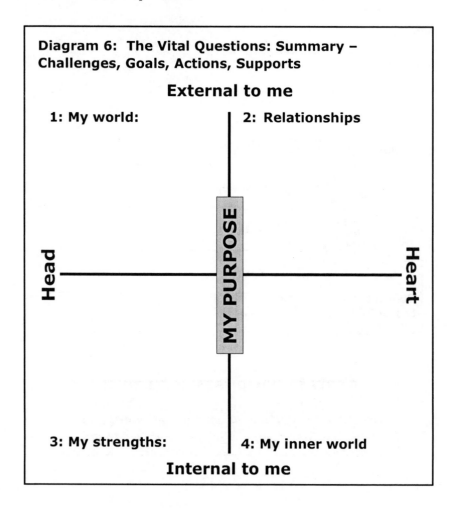

**Diagram 6: The Vital Questions: Summary –
Challenges, Goals, Actions, Supports**

External to me

1: My world:

2: Relationships

Head

MY PURPOSE

Heart

3: My strengths:

4: My inner world

Internal to me

Chapter 3

Telling your story

> *But we cannot live the afternoon of life according to the programme of life's morning – for what was great in the morning will be little at evening, and what in the morning was true will at evening have become a lie.*
>
> **Carl Jung**

A. Introduction

"Stories" are seen here as the personal beliefs and images that we have about ourselves and that we use to tell ourselves and the world who we are. "Why does this always happen to me?" for example suggests that the person saying this has a set of stories about how everything always goes wrong for them no matter what they do.

Or sometimes people tell the same story over and over again about a success they had many years ago and it becomes apparent that they are still trapped by their earlier success and haven't moved on since then.

So "stories" are not meant here as works of fiction or novels or something that only children tell but more how we have made sense of our personal history. And even if we think we are rational beings and immune from this then this "rationality" is our self-image and the "story" we tell about ourselves.

And the stories we tell? Stories about who we are and what made us the person we now are. A story can illustrate a particular characteristic or value of ours much more clearly than simply stating it as a fact. These stories let us and others know how people are likely to behave in different situations. (Interview questions are often around this, but they call it behavioural event interviewing instead of story telling.)

Other stories can be about our vision for what we would like to have happen or what we intend to do. Or teaching stories where we can draw a parallel between the story and our own experiences. With stories we can influence and create new ways of seeing for others – light bulb moments. *Aesop's Fables* for example are stories that give clear suggestions for ways people should act or their motives. (The story of the fox being unable to reach the grapes and then justifying his failure by saying they were probably sour is as relevant now as it was when Aesop wrote it.)

Stories can also be a great means of self-discovery. Telling our story to others enables us and them to see the patterns and themes in our lives. We can then decide as we become clearer about our patterns whether they are helping us or getting in our way.

Victim stories especially do us no favours. These are stories where people present themselves as powerless and at the mercy of others. The "gain" from the story is that the person never needs to take responsibility for his or her self. It is always someone else's fault. Byron Katie has a wonderful set of questions around these negative sorts of stories – is it true? Is it absolutely true? What is the effect of believing that? Who would you be if you didn't have that story?

And as an Inner Leader your stories are vitally important – the liberating stories are the ones to tell such as success epics. Foremost of all these is the epic of the Hero's Journey as described by Joseph Campbell.

Campbell, who spent a great deal of his life collecting myths from around the world, identified certain key phases in the journey of the leader. These involved firstly, an awareness that something was lacking in their life. This leads on to a rejection of this life; an alienation from society and the beginning of a journey to find the unknown "missing" aspect – be it a search for meaning or understanding, for knowledge or power, or love.

The journey stage involves great hardships and suffering. Often the hero has to battle against tremendous odds – sometimes even fight for their life: a battle which they may lose. This stage can also be a journey through a barren wilderness with no support or nourishment. If the leader survives this experience, he or she is transformed, gaining inner strength, wisdom and power. Once this change has occurred the leader is ready to move on to the next stage – the gaining of the prize, whatever it may be. After reaping the rewards he or she then return bearing their newfound knowledge and wisdom to the place where they started from – and use these gifts for the benefit of those they had left behind.

This is a story that all societies recognise about an ordinary person who is called to greatness – often in spite of themselves. In England the legends of King Arthur and the search for the Holy Grail is the best example of this. One of the reasons that the Harry Potter series is so popular is that it has very much the same themes. Ultimately of course each person's journey or story is unique. In King Arthur the knights all enter a forest where there is no clear path that they can see so they go their separate ways creating their own pathways. This is very similar to our lives. In other words we make up our own stories that are uniquely our own. And often these stories come from journeys through places we did not know we were going to go through.

When people tell their stories there are some universal themes and patterns. They have a determination to better themselves, to move beyond and above where they started, to make a difference. They often face difficulties because of their willingness to stand up for their beliefs, even when this leads to isolation and being cast into the wilderness. Hopefully their day then comes and they return to the fold bringing their skills and knowledge with them – along with self-belief and also humility.

This stage happens when a person is fully developed, rounded and mature. Often, the leaders we have are not paragons of virtue – they have not developed as they need to, and the companies, organisations or countries they lead suffer as a result. When King Arthur was physically and emotionally ill this was reflected in the suffering of England as a country. People lacked the sense of meaningfulness in their lives as exemplified by King Arthur.

We also need to be connected to stories to give meaning to our lives and work. In the East many tasks are seen as sacred; the cook in a Buddhist monastery for example is recognised as carrying out a noble calling.

The story of management consultants could be similar to the story of the Troubadours, roaming between organisations carrying information from one group to another and maybe cheering them up with a song (or the latest management fad). Life or business coaches can be seen as priests offering protected space so individuals can say what they really mean without fear.

One of the best analyses of modern management is by Martin Page in *The Corporate Savage*. He is essentially relating the stories that African tribes tell about themselves to the stories that modern leaders tell – and there is little difference.

Many recent leadership books have extolled the virtues of tribes in people's lives. This is something that Martin Page discussed many years ago. We are all "savages" which is not a term of abuse, but simply acknowledging our instincts, wherever we are, whatever we do, to act as part of a tribe. He gives many examples of the parallels between tribal life and corporate life which we ignore at our peril.

Those who think that organisational life is "rational" miss out on the essentials of organisational leadership. Take "tribal spirit" – it exists. The Ashanti of Ghana had a reputation for aggression as a tribe even though as individuals they were no different from others. This tribal spirit made them one of the most warlike and successful tribes in West Africa as happens with our more successful corporations.

The "tribal spirit" or organisational culture shapes individuals and what they do. If you look at many modern corporations their structures are very similar to those of tribal village life – with the Chief Executive, as in the tribe, having the most prestigious accommodation.

Martin Page also suggests that there is no real difference between consultants and witch doctors; both offer their clients a feeling of reassurance; that their "magic" works. The higher the fee, the greater the distance they come the more powerful is their magic. And the magic comes from their "stories" about their clients and their previous successes. So to succeed as an Inner Leader is to tell your story – in all its authenticity and truth – with passion, humour and humility

Exercise 13: What story represents you?

Think of the stories, legends, new or old, books, films, songs you know.

Which one most represents your personal story?

Which fictional character would you say you were most like – and why?

At which stage in the story are you?

What do you think will happen?

What insights do you recognise as helpful for you to understand your own story?

Favourite stories (Books, Films, Plays, Songs)

The characters you are most like and why

At which stage in the story are you?
What do you think will happen?

Key insights

B. Telling Your Story

Exercise 14: So what is your story? Using a Lifeline.

This is one of those exercises where it would be helpful to have someone to talk to: you tell them your story and ask them to see what patterns or themes emerge.

If you can't find someone then do the work yourself, but recognise it's not the easiest thing to be an observer of your own life story! Start with your own preparation first.

My life is like: (use an image/comparison or a plot/character from a story).

Lifeline

On a large sheet of paper (the larger the better) draw a line representing your life so far. Take a line and draw it for your life – from 0 to now – with highs and lows in whatever way you like (straight line, ups and downs, wavy etc.). Then use different coloured post-it notes for each of the following categories (feel free to add your own). Post these on the line.

Significant personal events

Feelings

Significant Others

Achievements at work

Key events in the world

You can add drawings, pictures, anything you want which has some meaning for you. Out of all this will come a self-portrait of you and your story.

Next, is to see what this all means. Answer the following (and if you can discuss this with a friend so much the better):

What themes or patterns are running through your life?

What are the values and key characteristics you have shown?

What are the different roles you have played and are playing?
Father/Mother, son, daughter, worker, manager, sportsperson, friend, etc.

What key beliefs do you have about the world, yourself and others which are displayed there? Many of these are laid down as small children, but emerge through our lives.

What insights occur to you as you look at your life patterns?

Themes and patterns

Values and personal characteristics

Roles

Key beliefs

Insights

C. Changing Your Story – Limiting Beliefs

As children we had to find ways of dealing with the strange and often threatening world around us. No matter how loving our parents were we had to learn for ourselves to deal with unpredictability and make our own sense of the world.

These patterns, although effective at the time, may be self-limiting for us as adults, especially as they will have strong emotional aspects through being formed in childhood. (Believing in Santa Claus still has a power for some people – waiting for a magic rescuer for example such as a wonderful new boss, politician or partner who will solve all their problems.)

As we meet our lifetime tasks of building self-identity, relating to others, making a living and developing a sense of our place in the world, our early discouragement can lead to us holding back or not being as effective as we would like to be.

To develop and grow we need encouragement to revisit these beliefs and move on from them. These negative beliefs show up in patterns or cycles such as the following:

Belief: I need to be strong as no-one will look after me.
Feeling: Fear.
Behaviour: I tough it out and won't ask for help.
Confirmation: Others see me as strong and brushing away help so leave me alone which confirms my belief that I need to be strong as no-one will look out for me.

Exercise 15: Finding Your Own Self-Limiting Beliefs

There are several options you can use to look at what beliefs are getting in your way. In all these only go as deep and share what you are happy with.

a) Reviewing the Past

Think about recent situations where you felt or thought you were not as effective as you would have liked to have been.

What were you thinking?
What were you feeling?
What were you doing?

And what are the beliefs that were holding you back or restricting you fully being yourself? What were you denying in yourself?

b) Shoulds and Musts (or Shouldn'ts and mustn'ts)

Work quickly and respond to these statements. Note as many answers as you like but only spend a minute or so on each item.

I must (please other people, make them happy, and do my duty...)
I should...
As a leader I must / should /mustn't / shouldn't...
Bad leaders are...
The problem with people is that they...
The world is...

See what, if any, themes are negative or come from beliefs that are negative underlying these statements.

```
────────────── Shoulds and Musts ──────────────
│                                                │
│                                                │
│                                                │
│                                                │
│                                                │
│                                                │
│                                                │
│                                                │
└────────────────────────────────────────────────┘
```

c) Fears

A quick way to get at our limiting beliefs is to look at our fears in a work/leadership situation. What are we most frightened of happening at work or when we are leading? Will people see us as incompetent? Will we make mistakes? Not succeed? Be disliked?

Think of a past, present or future situation where you had or have some anxiety at work. What are your fears? Most of us have concerns around being approved of, or not being in control or feeling threatened financially, emotionally or sometimes physically. Which of these needs is threatened by your fear? Again what negative or limiting beliefs or driver patterns emerge?

d) Self-beliefs

What are your negative thoughts or beliefs about yourself? I am lazy? Boring? People don't like me?

Sometimes people have too high estimates of their skills or strengths and these can limit them but in our culture most of us have had messages from others about how lacking we are in different areas. These need to be cleared and we need to be realistic about ourselves. Being realistic in this context means being much more positive and accepting of strengths! So complete the following…

I am not good enough for…
I can't…
I don't…
People think I am….
My main flaw is…

Again what negative or limiting beliefs or driver patterns emerge?

Self-beliefs

e) Addiction to Unhappiness

Sometimes we feel we have to hold self-limiting beliefs about ourselves because of messages from other people (parents, siblings, and friends) – you must be unhappy, upset about the world etc. It's expected of us. E.g. *with all the suffering in the world how can you be so selfish as to be happy.*

You will find that the media, politicians etc. focus relentlessly on these negative messages and we also pick up many from childhood. Can you identify what messages you are carrying that are not your own? Ones for example that you have inherited from your parents?

f) Drivers

Drivers are ways in which we respond to challenge or stress. They are systems of limiting beliefs that come from childhood patterns. These Drivers have positive aspects to them but under stress they can get in the way and we become ineffective. There are five main drivers (and may well be more!) Which ones do you identify with most? Eric Berne developed these in his books, most famously in *Games People Play.*

Drivers

I must:	Negative beliefs
Be Perfect	I must be right; others will laugh at me if I make a mistake; leaders must be all knowing.
Please People	People will only like me if I do what they want; love is scarce, I need people's approval; leaders mustn't upset others.
Be Strong	I must be in control; showing feelings is a sign of weakness, real leaders are tough.
Try Hard	Effort counts more than success; if I've tried then that's all that matters; I am not going to succeed whatever I do. Leaders are judged by the hours they put in – I must work harder than others.
Hurry Up	I want it yesterday – speed is of the essence. Why are we wasting time discussing things – just do it. Leaders think faster than anyone else.

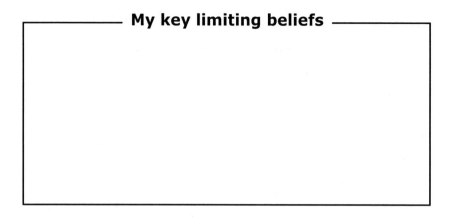

My key limiting beliefs

Exercise 16. Freeing Yourself from Negativity and Limitations

You may be feeling thoroughly miserable by now with all these drivers and negative beliefs washing around.

Worry not – they all have a positive side, fear keeps us out of danger for example. And we can change them! Not by resisting them *(What you resist persists)*, but by exploring the positive aspect and the origin of these beliefs and then gently changing them. Here is a range of options for you. And they do work.

a) Replace Drivers with Allowers

For each of the negative driver messages there is an antidote called Allowers.

Allowers

I must:	Antidote
Be Perfect	I am good enough as I am.
Please People	Please myself.
Be Strong	Be open and express my needs.
Try Hard	Just do it. (Don't worry about success – get on with it).
Hurry Up	Take my time and enjoy.

b) Positive Assumptions and Empowering Beliefs

Look at your negative beliefs and change the statements into positive ones such as:

I have all the time I need
Life is easy and fun
People are competent

Again what does this mean for you in practice?

b¹) The Incisive Question

Often there is one key question which if asked will get to the core of the issue. Nancy Kline (*Time to Think,* 1999, Ward Lock) suggests the following.

Ask yourself:
What am I assuming that is stopping me achieving my goal?
    (To find the core negative assumption)
What is my positive opposite of that assumption?
If I knew that new, freeing assumption, what ideas would I now have towards achieving my goal?

Make certain you use the exact words for the polar opposite and keep asking the question. New ideas will keep coming up. In the Incisive Question use the present tense when stating the new positive truth.

c) Change self-image

A very simple approach is to take any negative belief about yourself and phrase it in the past tense.

I used to believe I was (negative)...but now I know I am (positive).

d) Underlying needs

What are the underlying needs you are trying to meet through the negative belief cycle? E.g. If I am strong I will meet my need for being in control. Ask yourself:
Can I let go of WANTING approval, control or feeling safe?

Remember it is only the wanting that gets in the way. It's great to have approval, to be in control and feel safe – but if we want it this means we don't believe we have it. Let go of wanting and just accept you have it.

What does this mean for you in practice?

e) New Situations /Experimenting with changing negative beliefs

What situations are available for you to practise new behaviours that change negative beliefs? Situations that are fairly simple and not too important are best. E.g. If you always please others and put their wants before yours (negative belief – others' needs are more important than mine) then try stating your needs: *"I'd like to have lunch at 12.30 not 13.00"* for example.

f) Finding support

Most people find it difficult when someone else is changing – it threatens their own sense of competency. So you need to make certain you have a couple of supporters who will encourage you to move on and discard negative beliefs. So who will they be? Mentors and coaches are great but think of friends or colleagues too.

g) Letting go of negative feelings

If we feel anxious or upset as we let go of our negative beliefs (and it is like saying goodbye to old friends – albeit ones that we may have outgrown) then we need to deal with our feelings and emotions. Acknowledge these feelings and allow the energy in them to flow out and release. You may also like to say to yourself...

Could I let go of feeling...
Would I let go of feeling...
When? Now!

This simple but effective exercise is from the Sedona Method. You may need to repeat this cycle several times as you undertake to change long-held beliefs; but it will work at clearing guilt and other negatives.

The guilt feels real: *"Oh dear I was selfish and asked for what I wanted"* Nevertheless it is guilt based upon a false belief and so needs to be put aside.

Putting It Together

Now you are ready for the best bit – a positive belief cycle!

Belief: I can ask for help if there's something I can't do.
Feeling: Realistic self-confidence.
Behaviour: Asking for help positively when necessary.
Confirmation: Others are good at their stuff and I'm good at mine and we help and support each other.

My positive belief cycle

┌──────────── **New positive Belief** ────────────┐
│   │
│   │
│   │
│   │
│   │
└──┘

┌──────────── **New positive Feeling** ───────────┐
│   │
│   │
│   │
│   │
└──┘

New positive Behaviour

D. Creating a New Story

To change our lives we need to change our stories and our beliefs about ourselves. One of the best ways of doing this is Future Self visioning or storytelling.

This is seeing ourselves in a different story with things going the way we would prefer them to go. Other terms for this are "mental rehearsal" as used by top performers in sports and business. There are many techniques for doing this but one would be to pick a time in the future and see your Future Self being, feeling and acting as you would like them to.

You can then in your imagination from that perspective look back at where you are and imagine all the steps you had taken to get there. Then rewrite your story incorporating the Future Self. For example:

I decided to get up 30 minutes earlier everyday and eat a healthy breakfast. This led to me being more alert and energetic at work which then led my boss to suggest I take on extra responsibilities with a pay rise.

Exercise 17: Creating a New Story

Create a vision of your Future Self as you would like it to be. Describe this in detail. If you wish you can link this to exercise 8: My Dreams/Ideal Day exercise in the last chapter. (See Page 34).

Future Self Description

What habits and changes do you need to make NOW to reach the Future Self?

Changes

Write your new story (or if you prefer use pictures).

New Story

Put in place a way of checking every day that you are going in the right direction with this new story. And make a list of all your positive gains! Checks and Gains: e.g. I know I am going in the right direction because...

Checks and Gains

E. Deeper Issues with Our Stories

Many of us have deeper and more traumatic issues in our histories. But we can get help. For example one of the most successful processes is Matrix Reimprinting, based on Emotional Freedom Techniques, which can help people reframe deeply traumatic events in their past – especially from when they were children. Do not lose sight of the fact that for many people support from mates and friends is all that is needed.

One example is addiction. Jack Trimpey who used to have issues with drinking has written *Rational Recovery* with some controversial views expressed in it. He is all for us accepting we have a choice. As he says we all choose to be dependent on different chemicals: addiction is when we want to give the substance up, but are ambivalent about it.

We're not sure of how we want our story to go. We enjoy the gains from the addiction as well as accepting the downsides and it's ultimately a choice whether we change or not. Not something that many people would agree with!

However, it fits in with the willingness model of addictive behaviour, back to Socrates over two thousand years ago. Socrates thought we want to choose what is good, but things which tempt us make us see them in that moment as the best choice and so we continue with the addiction. The key point in all of this is to recognise that our behaviours and choices come from our limiting beliefs. For example:

I'll never succeed in losing weight – is a limiting belief,

but it can be changed to something more positive:

I can do it if I choose to do.

F. Finding Your Voice

At the core of becoming a leader is the need always to connect one's voice and one's touch. There is of course a prior task -finding one's voice in the first place
Max De Pree, *Leadership Jazz*

The voice throws us back on what we want for our life. It forces us to ask ourselves who is speaking? Who came to work today? Who is working for what? What do I really care about?
David Whyte, *The Heart Aroused*

65

Out of all these stories you have been examining there is one thing that is key:

You are a unique individual with your own story to tell,
    in your own way and with your own unique voice.
Your voice comes from your own being and is special to you.

This is also known as presence or charisma and we all have it or can develop it.

Exercise 18: Finding Your Voice

What is unique and special and precious about you?

And how can you express this in your own unique way – your voice?

Expressions of your unique voice

A leader's voice is really a chorus. Voice is a noun and a verb.
Voice lessons are essential to leadership development.
Voice is the echo of beliefs. You find your voice in all the places you left it
J Kouzes

66

Chapter 4

Being your Best

Success in the knowledge economy comes to those who know themselves -their strengths, their values, and how they best perform.
First and foremost, concentrate on your strengths. Put yourself where your strengths can produce results.
Second, work on improving your strengths. Analysis will rapidly show where you need to improve skills or acquire new ones.
Third, discover where your intellectual arrogance is causing disabling ignorance and overcome it. It is equally essential to remedy your bad habits – the things you do or fail to do that inhibit your effectiveness and performance. At the same time, feedback will also reveal when the problem is a lack of manners. Manners are the lubricating oil of an organisation.

Peter Drucker
"Managing Oneself" Harvard Business Review March-April 1999.

A. Living a Fulfilled Life – Achieving Your Potential

A fulfilled life can be defined as continuously developing in order to reach your full potential – whatever that may be. Anything which helps people move towards attaining that potential is "good"; anything that blocks it is "bad". Obviously as everyone is unique their potential and what they need to do to attain it will be highly personal. This isn't a matter of position or status. Anyone, whatever their situation, age or background, can open themselves up to this process.

The latest thinking in positive psychology reinforces much of this. Happiness comes from learning and growing and focusing on others rather than on your own wishes. Aristotle saw leisure activities as a means of refreshing oneself, but he also saw certain types of work as having the same effect. It, therefore, isn't a question of work-life balance; rather how you approach your work and the use you make of your leisure time that counts

In order to become your best you need to know what you have the potential to be great at and where your interests lie. You can become clear about this in several ways. (You also need to be aware of the areas where you are not so good – your Shadow which will be looked at later in the chapter.)

Exercise 19A: Identifying Your Best Self
– Your own point of view

Being your best doesn't mean being perfect. "Good enough" is the focus. For example if you were the most perfect parent ever your children would forever be living in your shadow.

"Best self" is about being human and whole rather than shining clean without any blemishes. So bearing that in mind what are your views on your potential?

You may want to go back to the Strengths part of the Vital Questions in Chapter 2 (see Page 30) to remind yourself of some of your strengths.

Also you might find it useful to look at the "Bragging" questions from the website "http://www.bragbetter.com".

When I'm at my best, I'm...

Exercise 19B: Identifying Your Best Self
– Others' Feedback

Ask three others (more if you want) to give you feedback on when they have seen you at your best or what they value most about you. They need to be specific and give you examples. And absolutely no suggestions for improvements.

Many people find this a tough exercise for themselves. We are so used to hearing about how we could be better it's sometimes hard to hear and believe what people value about us.

1: Other's Feedback on my Best Self

2: Other's Feedback on my Best Self

3: Other's Feedback on my Best Self

Other Sources of Feedback

There are hundreds of questionnaires available to help you to identify your strengths, including the respected and well established Myers-Briggs Type Inventory. Others available online that are helpful include:

The VIA Inventory of Strengths: "http://www.viastrengths.org", which measures 24 character strengths and gives you a free feedback report on your top five character strengths.

The Clifton StrengthsFinder: "http://www.strengthsfinder.com", which measures 34 themes and gives you a feedback report on your top five themes of talent. However, to access the Clifton StrengthsFinder, which is owned by The Gallup Organisation in the United States, you need to purchase a book that includes a StrengthsFinder access code (either of the two Clifton books in the bibliography at the end of this book have this, or you can find further details at their website.

Exercise 19c: Identifying Your Best Self
– Pulling it all Together

So, summing it all up...

┌──────────────── **Your Best Self is:** ────────────────┐
│   │
│   │
│   │
│   │
│   │
│   │
└──┘

B. Am I doing what I do best? Developing a Practice

A "Practice" is a discipline of daily life aimed at improving one's skills or character. It is most evident in sports – the committed athlete for example. To be a great athlete the individual will study past performances of other great athletes, their performance and techniques; more importantly he will apply the same level of discipline to himself and to his practice for maximum improvement.

An essential part of the practice is getting feedback from others; another, equally important, is accepting that there are rules and standards of excellence in the chosen field – and abiding by those rules and standards. The individual can't just dismiss feedback or change the rules if he doesn't like them. And so to become our best we need to choose and follow a practice ourselves.

So specifically a practice involves:

Commitment and passion

Standards of excellence and accepting the authority of these standards

A history and body of knowledge about the area that is being practised

A community of teachers and learners

As a participant accepting others' authority

Feedback on these standards

If we are to be our best we must make certain that we have the chance in our daily lives, whether at work or in leisure to put into practice the things we love doing and we are good at. As Aristotle said: *"Excellence is a habit"*. Matthew Seyd in *Bounce* talks about the need for self-directed practice and he and Malcolm Gladwell (*Outliers*) reckon that the truly great spend about 10,000 hours practising their craft. Of course if you love what you're doing the hours will fly by! One of the best ways of developing ourselves is to establish a practice with others who are equally committed to getting better at what they do.

For some people their work is their life and their life their work. This may not be true for all of us, but we can still aim to give of our best – especially those of us who have the privilege to be leaders. Surely any leader would want to improve their skills, develop excellence and commit to daily improvement? But how many leaders do we see who are committed to this in the same way as an enthusiastic sportsperson?

As with sports practices so with leadership. There are guidelines and standards – not as clearly defined in sports but they are there. There are authorities in the form of "good" leaders; we study these to learn from them.

As in a sport, we know that imitation won't work; we have to learn and adapt points to our own unique leadership style. We need to practise leadership and to be continuously open to feedback on what works and what doesn't. We need to talk about leadership with others, whether more formally as in leadership seminars or over a coffee break.

In the search for our inner leader, we rely on others, more expert than we are, to teach us strategies; to evaluate our work and suggest improvements; to answer our questions and to encourage and guide us. At the same time as we develop these skills, we need to be able to recognise and value those skills in others. It has long been accepted that the "authorities" or "keepers" of leadership practices and standards are the business schools; but when it comes to *applied* leadership, we are best served by learning from those who practise it every day, on the ground, in the work place.

The importance of conversations

In developing our leadership skills, we learn best by listening and interacting with others: namely, through conversations. Such conversations may be formal, as in mentoring or coaching sessions; but the most effective and successful areas of learning are in the informal interactions we have on a daily basis – such as routine meetings, discussions over coffee, brief exchanges with co-workers and neighbours.

It is conversations which allow us to grow and develop ourselves; and it is through conversations we are able to practise leadership to change and improve our organisations.

Exercise 20: Starting a "Practice"

Setting up a "Practice" Group.

Which of your strengths are you looking to develop?

Whom will you trust to support and challenge you?

How will you go about setting up a daily practice for this?

How will you measure progress?

C. Focusing on the Positive

A search for the capabilities and possibilities in people
is gradually supplanting the search for the liabilities.
It is a more optimistic philosophy.
Robert Greenleaf

Many people are conditioned to focus on the negative by their parents, their friends and general attitudes in society. Even some forms of therapy ask clients to focus on what went wrong as a child and then expect them to become happy as a result!

Human Givens, also a form of therapy, suggests that this is the way to depression and instead gets people to relax and focus on the positive outcomes. What this does is create new behaviours allowing us to create the future from our future aims and goals instead of being anchored in the past. To use an analogy: focusing on the negative past is like driving by only looking in the rear view mirror instead of looking at the road ahead and driving towards our destination.

The emphasis on the positive is the best way to help people to change. By developing this "yes" approach people and organisations can change easily and enthusiastically. It is often so much easier and requires less effort to say yes than to block with nos.

Excellent teams, for example, have a ratio of at least 3 to 6 positive comments for every negative remark. So focus on what you want yourself (and others) to do rather than what not to do!

As an example one emergency hospital unit in the USA got rid of over a hundred negative signs and procedures and replaced them with positive requests or suggestions – including having the security guards be helpful. Within one month of reducing negative cues, the ER experienced a one-third decline in customer complaints. Contrast this with the majority of signs that you see around you in everyday life.

It is also salutary to be aware of our own negative language habits: how often do we complain or focus on the negative instead of praising the positive? And this applies even more to ourselves: the majority of people are their own worst critics. So try changing this to positive appreciation.

Exercise 21: Saying Yes: Appreciation and Evaluation

———— A Checklist for every day ————

	Wonderful	Superb	Magnificent	Fantastic	Incredible
How magnificent was I today?					
How open was I towards my own learning and development?					
Who else was magnificent? Have I told them?					

Name:

_____

Appreciation:

_____

——— What have I said "Yes" to today? ———

Area:	Action:

D. The Shadow

Our deepest fears are like dragons guarding our deepest treasure.
Rainer Maria Rilke

If you don't break your ropes while you're alive
Do you think ghosts will do it after?
Kabir

A. The Shadow in Ourselves

Now of course everyone is not perfect. We all have "Shadows". The Shadow is that part of us which we have no wish to be; the part we reject because of our fears of what we have hidden in there. There are many chunks in most people of "frozen terror".

These usually come from childhood traumas whether big or small. The ego locks down and restricts our natural life energy because of these fears – and we become cautious and fearful in the present.

Transmuting these barriers to allow your natural power to flow is key to Inner Leadership. Following the concept of appreciation and evaluation you can think of the Shadow as hiding your "Inner Gold".

Your task is to identify the many levels of challenge you face within your Shadow and to work through them to your best self. Discovering your best self is your true purpose.

So, how do you uncover your Shadow? One way is to look at the limiting beliefs we all have which were discussed in the previous chapter such as:

I'm worthless
Others are better than me
I can't....
I'm unlovable...
People always leave me

The Shadow also harbours our deepest fears. It's essential if you look at these to have people around you who can offer support, if necessary. What are we most frightened of that we or others will find out about ourselves?

"Overcoming our Shadow" means confronting our deepest fears. This is often taxing and difficult. Do we dislike others because they present the very characteristics we most fear in ourselves?

If this part of the process of developing our inner leader sounds tough, perhaps almost unendurable, then take heart: the energy liberated, the knowledge acquired of our true self means that working with our Shadow is like being let out of prison: a prison whose bars prevent us from being fully ourselves.

Having identified your deepest fears, you can develop techniques to overcome them, to uncover the Inner Gold within them. An excellent start is Reframing, in which you turn every negative belief about yourself or others to its positive opposite. For example: 'they are overly critical' becomes 'they have exceptionally high standards'. Simply see the best in every negative belief about yourself or others.

You can also try befriending your Shadow. Remember the saying "What you resist persists"? So for example the next time you experience pain, instead of fighting or moving away from it, try *welcoming* it, as if it were a trusted friend with unpleasant, but important news.

Exercise 22: Your Shadow

What qualities do I fear or dislike in myself? (A good way in is to think of people you dislike or to read the exact opposite psychological profile of yourself).

Shadow qualities?

How can I work with these to find the Inner Gold within me?

b) The Shadow at Work

It is common to see the Shadow at work. Bullies, workaholics, perfectionists are all showing their Shadow side.

Organisations have Shadows too; some charities and religious groups behave in ways that seem opposite to their professed values.

Whenever control is seen as essential and people made to follow rules strictly without regard to human nature you can bet that someone's Shadow is in charge. They are shielding themselves by using power (or money or status) to disguise their fear of being seen as weak or worthless or inadequate.

Inner Leaders need to make certain that they are not caught up in the Shadows of others, especially organisational Shadows.

It is easy just to accept what everyone says about blaming others and finding scapegoats instead of looking honestly at oneself and taking responsibility for one's own faults.

For example blaming politicians and bankers for all the faults of the financial crisis without recognising that it is something for which we all share a degree of responsibility through the use of readily available credit.

c) Stress and Burnout

That which does not kill me makes me stronger
Nietzsche

Stress and anxiety are common; they are also sensible reactions to the world around us. It helps to think of them as messages suggesting that we need to do something about a situation or a relationship. Many of us over-react; the present brings up past traumas (big or small) and this energy can be overwhelming.

Stress is our reaction to events, internal or external when we feel we are not capable of meeting their challenge. This often raises some of the limiting beliefs we have about ourselves; I'm not good enough etc.

However, there is good news. Through a range of techniques including meditation, self-awareness, action, and support from others, we can let go of most of the baggage we are carrying from the past and focus on the present.

Many of us though, again quite logically, try to solve stress issues with our usual preferred methods of actions; but these often are the problem in themselves. For example if we always run away from conflict, in the short term this will save us stress, but sooner or later we will have to deal with it – and the pressure may then be much more intense.

Burnout is different from stress. Burnout happens when we overdo some activity in our lives; it takes over to the extent of wiping out variety and balance. Overworking is the most common form of burnout; but obsessive physical exercise or any obsessive activity can also cause burnout. The best solution is to find an alternative activity which you enjoy – and, most importantly, which is completely different from the source of the burnout.

Exercise 23. Stress

Think of something that causes you stress. What is the trigger point? What is the effect on you? What do you do about it

Cause of Stress:	Its effect on you:

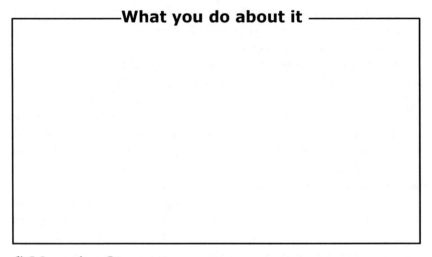

d) Managing Stress

> *To laugh often and much; to win the respect of intelligent people and the affection of children; to earn the appreciation of honest critics and endure the betrayal of false friends; to appreciate beauty, to find the best in others; to leave the world a bit better, whether by a healthy child, a garden patch or a redeemed social condition; to know even one Life has breathed easier because you have lived.*
> **This is to have succeeded.**
>
> **Ralph Waldo Emerson**

There are several techniques to help you to manage stress and move towards inner peace, courage and appreciation.

The Sedona Method, for example, allows you let go of fears and negative emotions. It also helps you identify true "wants" from false "wants", so you can be clear on what it is you are seeking, and thus concentrate your energy in positive directions.

Another method is the Emotional Freedom Technique which also helps people to dissolve past fears and worries. This, combined with Matrix Reimprinting, takes people back to the times when stress occurred and helps them to overcome the sources of stress. Even more importantly it is very successful in helping them to change any negative beliefs about themselves or the world.

There are many such techniques; the important thing is to explore which of them works best for you. However, some general guidelines for stress management are applicable to everyone.

They include:

Balance work, leisure, social and family
 – don't let work intrude into home.

Learn to set sensible, realistic targets
 and be able to say **"NO!"**

Look after your body, emotions and mind.
 Exercise; keep yourself in positive relationships, and look for mental stimulation.

Look for the positive.
 What is this situation teaching me? What do I enjoy?

Reward yourself for things done well.

Know your own capacity
 – energy, concentration etc.

Don't be too tough on yourself.

Laugh
 – see the humour.

Have a "wellness" strategy
 – enough sleep, good food, rest and exercise.

Leisure activities that absorb us in which we lose track of time seem to be critical in "bouncing back" from being stressed.

Almost anything can be regarded as 'leisure', as Mihaly Csikszentmihaly in *Beyond Boredom and Anxiety* makes clear:

"The results suggest that anything one does can become rewarding if the activity is structured right and if one's skills are matched with the challenges of the action. In this optimal condition people enjoy even work, extreme danger and stress. To change a boring situation into one that provides its own reward does not require money or physical energy; it can be achieved through symbolic restructuring of information." (*Changing your view of it!*)

Exercise 24: My Stress Management Commitment

This is what I will do to reduce stress in my life...

Physical: My "wellness strategy

Emotional: turning "negative" feelings into positive/ identifying my emotional needs and how I can fulfill

Social: intimacy, friends, support, fun

Mental: balance of stimulation and relaxation

Chapter 5

Companions

A. Why do we need companions?

Love is the dynamism that infallibly brings the unconscious to light.

Carl Jung

Love may be all we need but there are many ways of expressing this. We all to some extent need companions, some more than others of course, to share our lives.

All of us need:

To be noticed and belong

To be in control (or sometimes to have others control us)

To be liked or loved

Now everyone will vary enormously in the strengths of their needs in the above areas and for that reason understanding the unique pattern for each of us can take a lot of discussion and insight. To add to the complexity people often confuse their needs.

Many people don't know how to love or be loved and so try to get this through control (or sometimes try to get control by getting others to like them). Or, as Don Juan tried, going from person to person trying to find intimacy, but running away when it appears through fear of being trapped.

All this rich interplay of needs makes for the complex patterns of relationships that make up families, friends, organisations and societies. In many ways even work organisations can be seen as simply means for people to try to get their personal needs met. Hence why we need companions; people we share our work and lives with. Recognising these essential needs, both in ourselves and in others, means that they can be met more easily and conflict minimised.

The Inner Leader understands his or her own needs as well as those of other people and helps them to achieve them. Love is not often spoken about in work or leadership yet it is as vital a motivation as any other, and for most people, the most important. Without the flow of love we shrivel and die. It takes courage to demonstrate love, respect, and concern for others instead of sheltering behind our roles or status. As an Inner Leader we need to overcome the barriers we have to sharing our love and expressing our true loving self.

So what do you need from others? Significance (belonging), control or approval? Non-Violent Communication, for example, is a process that can help us to uncover ours and others' needs by developing empathy towards ourselves and listening to ourselves and likewise to others.

Exercise 25: What I need in relationships

Which of the needs along the top do you want to be met in each of the arenas of relationships and in what priority?

	Significance – belonging	Feeling in control	Being loved Approval
Intimate relationships			
Family			
Friends			
Work colleagues			

How well are these needs being met?

	What is being met?	Would like more/ less of...
Intimate relationships		
Family		
Friends		
Work colleagues		

So, overall, what do I need to focus on?

B. Building Relationships

Leaders express their role through relationships. It is the quality of these relationships that determines how they will be seen as a leader. Sometimes of course difficult decisions have to be made, but the Inner Leader focuses on the ultimate welfare of their people when making these tough decisions.

Relationships are also seen as an end in themselves not just as a means to get things done. Companions are valued for their own sake, not as a means to an end. Therefore, high quality relationships are essential to an Inner Leader. The Inner Leader will want to make certain that they are doing all they can to maintain and improve these relationships and to help others to meet their needs and improve their relationships in turn.

Different societies and different people will place emphasis on different aspects of relationships, as the last exercise showed. However, there do seem to be some universal rules. For example, in intimate relationships most people, regardless of gender, seem to want their partners to express their feelings more and be more appreciative. Some key guidelines follow, but remember to always allow for the uniqueness of each person in terms of their needs for significance, control or affection.

Learn practical social skills – how to ask questions, how to listen (absolutely key), how to acknowledge what the other person feels without being judgemental. This would include being sensitive to other cultures, races and faiths.

To start with, be clear what you and the other person want from the relationship. Is it temporary, transactional or deeper and longer lasting?

Give compliments, praise, show affection (again, depending on the relationship needs, this will vary) and use positive body language, facial signals, voice, to show liking.

Build self-esteem and mutual respect, concern for others, loyalty and commitment.

Be open, use self-disclosure, trust and confide in others.

Acknowledge birthdays and special events.

Exercise 26: People Mapping

To clarify what you and others want from your mutual relationships it is helpful to make a relationship map. Include all significant relationships, past and present, positive and negative. The aim is to look at the health of these relationships and see what actions, if any, need to be taken.

Plot all those people on paper around a small circle (you) in the middle. Those closer to that circle (you) are those you engage with the most. Also connect others to you with lines – the thicker the line the more important the connection. You can add scores out of ten if you so wish for enjoyment of that particular relationship. And then ask:

Who supports and motivates me?

Who drains and undermines me?

You could indicate the positive relationships with one colour and the negative with another colour. Then see what actions you can or cannot take to improve the quality of these relationships.

For example if you have an important connection with someone, but they are far away you might like to get closer to them. If people are draining you then protect yourself or move away.

If you have a strong relationship with someone in terms of interactions (thick close line), but enjoyment is low this can be a source of stress and again actions need to be taken.

Diagram 7. People mapping

PERSON A:
Enjoy 7/10,
but too distant.
Supports.
Action:
Invite for a
drink, meal
etc.

YOU

PERSON B:
Enjoy 2/10.
Drains.
Action:
Minimise
meetings

**People in
this
category:**

**People in
this
category:**

Those in-between:

C. Networking

Networking is seen either as something selfish or essential depending on your attitude. A survey of "lucky" people found that they took advantage (in a good way) of people they knew. For example, in a study of New York unemployed people it was found that those who would talk to others when in self-wash laundries were far more able to find jobs for themselves.

At work we need contacts to get information simply to do our everyday tasks. Other networks are equally important – networks of friends or acquaintances for finding out what's happening or sharing skills and knowledge.

Connections get us our reputation and we learn and make judgements about others on this same basis. And reciprocity rules here – if we get help, we need to offer help back. So thinking about your networks (use the people mapping exercise you've just done) complete the following exercise

Exercise 27: My Networking Strengths

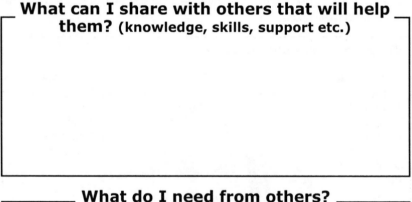

What can I share with others that will help them? (knowledge, skills, support etc.)

What do I need from others?
(knowledge, skills, support etc.)

What are my best networking strengths?
(communication skills, empathy, knowledge etc.)

What will I do now?

D. Leading Others

Best friend at work
Overall, just 30% of employees report having a best friend at work.
If you are fortunate enough to be in this group, you are seven times as likely to be
engaged in your job. Our results also suggest that people without a best friend at
work all but eliminate their chances of being engaged during the workday.
People with at least three close friends at work were 96% more likely
to be extremely satisfied with their life.
Gallup

Gallup research has shown that having a best friend at work dramatically improves productivity, engagement and retention. We can measure our needs and our behaviours in terms of relationships in a number of ways. Simply talking to people or using relationship questionnaires for example, can give us an indication of how important – or not – work relationships are to us.

There is no question that this is an extremely important area and one that is often neglected – certainly in Anglo-Saxon cultures with their focus on task. The exceptions show how effective investing in relationships can be. South-West Airlines in the US, which at one time was worth more than all the other US Airlines in terms of its market capitalisation invests heavily in relationships both within its organisation (staff) and outside (customers and suppliers)

Another study from the Centre for Creative Leadership in the USA found that the popular assumption about managers (that they are high on a need to express control) was wrong. The single factor that differentiated the top performing managers from the bottom managers was *expressed affection*.

Contrary to the popular myth of the cold-hearted boss who cares very little about people's feelings, the highest performing managers show more warmth and fondness toward others. They get closer to people and they are significantly more open in sharing thoughts and feelings than their lower performing counterparts.

These managers were not without their rational sides. In fact, they all scored high on "thinking," and they all scored high on their need to have power and influence over others. It is just that these factors didn't explain why managers were higher performers.

So leading others is about investing in relationships with our fellow workers and understanding their needs (There are several questionnaires which can help us to understand people's needs as well as our own, but really all that is needed is the ability to listen to others.)

Our Inner Leader understands that we need to vary our style depending on the person in front of us. Sometimes people need clear guidance; at other times just to be listened to or at other times to be left alone. This ability to adjust styles appropriately is a key skill of a coach and essential to Inner Leadership as well.

One revealing exercise is to see how we have duplicated our family relationships at work. Eg. Does our boss behave like one of our parents? And do we treat our co-workers like our siblings?

Politics is a great arena to see these dynamics played out. Politicians acting like parent figures for example instead of brothers or sisters helping other family members. Often there is someone in the family who carries the Shadow as a scapegoat for everyone else. Women often carry it for men and vice versa.

We need to differentiate between these and stop disliking someone because they remind us of someone with whom we had problems when we were at school!

One way to review our relationships at work is to think of them in terms of emotional savings accounts. Instead of money the currency is the feeling of mutual trust and respect that people have for each other.

Positive deposits come from: keeping promises, caring about others, helping them with their work or problems, showing appreciation, listening

Withdrawals or debits come from: not keeping promises, criticising others unfairly or in front of others, not admitting when you have made mistakes, or ignoring others concerns.

Build trust through monitoring your "Emotional Bank Account" with others and identify what you do or say that might cause others to lose their respect for you or to start to distrust you.

Show appreciation, especially for the "small stuff". Recognise effort and treat others with kindness and respect including bosses. Saying "Thank you" to a colleague for a favour or appreciating anything that's done to help beyond the call of duty are good places to start.

Exercise 28: Emotional Bank Accounts

Your Emotional Bank Account			
Individual	Credit/Positive Deposits	Debit/ Withdrawals	Balance +/-

E. Balancing Masculine and Feminine energies

For one human being to love another;
that is perhaps the most difficult task of all...,
the work for which all other is preparation.
It is a high inducement to the individual to ripen...
a great exacting claim upon us,
something that chooses us out and calls us to vast things.
Rainer Maria Rilke

Perhaps the easiest way to look at masculine and feminine energies is to use the Chinese idea of yin and yang. Yin is soft receptive energy (pull) and yang is hard, expressive energy (push). We all, regardless of our sex, have both of these energies and we need them both to be successful.

Carl Jung coined the terms Anima and Animus. The anima is the feminine aspect of a man and can represent his ideal woman – likewise the animus is the masculine part of a woman. All of us, regardless of our sexual orientation have these two components.

Having only yin energy would mean we never can do anything and exist as perpetual victims subject to others. Having only yang would lead to a total lack of empathy and pure action without reflection.

When we think of communication the two types of energy become apparent. Yin is about listening and receiving, yang about expression and assertiveness. Put these together and we get an idea of our communication style.

No one area is better than the others. There are times when it's best to be quiet and occasions when we just need to tell others what we think.

We can start thinking of flows of energies rather than being restricted to stereotypes of what men and women are expected to be. This can be very freeing for people as they realize that they do not have to conform to society's expectations of gender.

Use the table on the next page to identify your favourite style and examine the advantages and disadvantages of that particular style and explore what, if anything, you need to do to develop other styles.

Diagram 8. Communication styles

Expressiveness
(Yang)

1: POWER

Driver

2: FRIENDSHIP

Conversationalist

Non-Receptive
(Low Yin)

Receptive
(Yin)

Non-communication

3: ACHIEVEMENT

Receiver

4: EMPATHY

(Low Yang)
Non-Expressiveness

Exercise 29: My Communication Style

What is my favourite style?

Advantages and Disadvantages of this style?

The pluses

The minuses

Your balanced judgement

What do I need to develop?

F. Your People Plan – Cultivating Companionship

> *Your unconscious wants to entangle you in the thick web of relations*
> *that is the essence of human flourishing.*
> *It longs and begs for love.*
>
> **David Brooks,** *The Social Animal*

Being clear about your needs, networking and communication styles and having a people map is the beginning of understanding how to develop relationships, but it's not enough.

You need intention, acceptance of yourself and others without judging; and you need skills – especially empathetic listening which is the most valuable communication skill of all.

Your people plan should be very simple: pick one person every week, practise accepting them as they are without trying to change or control them and let go of judging them. You might want to see if you can get to ten out of ten for acceptance. Any barriers that might stop you from seeing them as a person in their own right will eventually dissolve.

And a great person to start with is you!

Can you accept yourself fully? Are you ready to be you fully in spite of all the messages which you had received as a child (and possibly even now) that you are not OK – that you need to be fixed? Can you let go of the barriers that you have put in place to stop you being you fully for fear of rejection? Good enough is good enough; perfection is frightening.

Ultimately, as Eric Berne put it, the aim is quite simple – getting to a place of: I'm OK – You're OK.

This means accepting yourself and others as you and they are – flawed, but human and all companions on the journey together.

Chapter 6

Leading in Organisations

Organisations, like people, have values.
To be effective in an organisation, a person's values must be compatible with the
organisation's values. They do not need to be the same, but they must be close
enough to coexist. Otherwise, the person will not only be frustrated but also will
not produce results. Values, in other words, are and should be the ultimate test.

Peter Drucker
Managing Oneself, **Harvard Business Review, March-April 1999.**

A. The Ideal Organisation for You

There is considerable research to show that we all have definite organisational preferences based on our personalities. In other words organisations have the culture they do because of the personalities of the people who have power in those organisations.

We need to understand that this is the key factor in the way organisations are structured. Business logic does, of course, play a part, but it is not as important as personality preferences in spite of what leaders will say when they attempt to justify their action. We need to understand what type of organisations suit different personalities and then, depending on our preferences, what is the right one for us.

Organisations can be classified in terms of their focus. Some organisations are very focused on tasks and production with issues such as quality and efficiency. These organisations tend to be predominant in manufacturing.

The marketing led organisations such as Unilever, Proctor and Gamble, Coca-Cola and Pepsi Cola define their successes in terms of market share and growth. In those industries it is all about expansion with the product being a means to an end.

There are not many people-focused organisations in industry – however some exist: a prime goal of TDI Industries, a Texas based air-conditioning firm, is to provide career opportunities for its staff. And there are a few creative type organisations such as small PR/market research companies.

The different focus of organisations leads to different ways of structuring and running the organisation. Production-centred organisations tend to have clear and strictly adhered to processes to ensure efficiency and quality whereas client-focused organisations will be more flexible so as to meet client needs.

This doesn't always happen of course and there are always exceptions to the rule. For example the worst client-focused organisations are bureaucratic in the extreme with service being subjected to inflexible processes.

As a generalisation we can classify these different types of organisation into the diagram below.

Again, there is a distinction between those organisations which are focused on the outer world of the market and clients and those that are more focused inwardly on processes and staff. We can make a further distinction between the focus on task and focus on people and this gives a broad classification of four types.

No organisation is just one of these types. All organisations need to cover all these areas otherwise they will fail, but we are looking at their main focus.

Diagram 9: Organisational focus

1. Market focused	**EXTERNAL**	2. Client focused
TASK	**Organisational goals and purpose**	PEOPLE
3. Production focused	**INTERNAL**	4. Employee focused

Exercise 30. My Ideal Organisation

For each of the statements in the next diagram allocate 10 points between them for what you think would be the perfect organisation for you.

E.g. 1. Organisational values should be:

Competitive and expansive	2
Responsive to clients and society	2
Competent and Efficient	1
Caring and helpful	5
= 10 points in total	

My Ideal Organisation (i)

EXTERNAL

1. Market focused

☐ **Organisation's values:** Competitive and expansive

☐ **Key Purpose:** Market Leader

☐ **Structure:** Flexible enough to attain goals

☐ **Process Focus:** Maximising delivery

☐ **Communication:** Based on need to know

☐ **Individuality:** Seen in wider context of organisation purpose

☐ **Rewards based on:** Achievement of objectives

☐ **Decision-making:** Appraisal of potential options

☐ **Relationships:** Open enough to get work done

☐ **Success Criteria:** Market share

TOTAL = ☐

3. Production focused

☐ **Organisation's values:** Competent and Efficient

☐ **Key Purpose:** Be productive and efficient

☐ **Structure:** Clearly defined

☐ **Process Focus:** Skills and expertise

☐ **Communication:** Dependent on work flows

☐ **Individuality:** Respected but subordinated to work

☐ **Rewards based on:** Performance and competency

☐ **Decision-making:** Objective analysis of facts

☐ **Relationships:** Fairly impersonal – work is key

☐ **Success Criteria:** Return on assets

TOTAL = ☐

My Ideal Organisation (ii)

INTERNAL

2. Client focused

- ☐ **Organisation's values:** Responsive to clients and society
- ☐ **Key Purpose:** Satisfy stakeholders
- ☐ **Structure:** Open and decentralised
- ☐ **Process Focus:** Developing individuals
- ☐ **Communication:** Totally open regardless of "status"
- ☐ **Individuality:** Encouraged and developed
- ☐ **Rewards based on:** Allowing for individual flair
- ☐ **Decision-making:** Individual insight and judgement
- ☐ **Relationships:** Whatever people want them to be
- ☐ **Success Criteria:** Contribution to society

TOTAL = ☐

4 Employee focused

- ☐ **Organisation's values:** Caring and helpful
- ☐ **Key Purpose:** Keep organisational members satisfied
- ☐ **Structure:** Well organised, but friendly
- ☐ **Process Focus:** Working with others effectively
- ☐ **Communication:** Based on good relationships
- ☐ **Individuality:** Respected within teams
- ☐ **Rewards based on:** People's seniority or position
- ☐ **Decision-making:** Sounding out of people's views
- ☐ **Relationships:** Personal, friendly and social
- ☐ **Success Criteria:** How people are treated

TOTAL = ☐

Now count up your totals for each quadrant. This should tell you where your preferences lie.

Market Focus = ☐

Client Focus = ☐

Production Focus = ☐

Employee Focus = ☐

What are your preferences in terms of structure and organisational culture?

And what does it mean to you?

How does your organisation compare to your preferences?

You can repeat the exercise above, but allocate scores on what you think the organisation IS instead of what you would prefer.

What, if anything, can you do about this?

B. Leading in Organisations

Large political and social organisations must not be ends in themselves, but merely temporary expedients. From the moment they grow beyond man and escape his control he becomes their victim and is sacrificed to the madness of an idea that knows no master. All great organisations in which the individual no longer counts are exposed to this danger.

Carl Jung.

Developing Inner Leadership

"So a company cannot be regarded merely as a production unit, any more than an African tribe can. Some are run exclusively for profit, but an amazing number are not. And these are indeed to be compared with an African tribe that produces In order to survive."

Martin Page

The Inner Leader understands that organisations exist for and through people rather than as an abstract entity to which people are sacrificed. One of the most insightful books on leaders is *Leadership without Easy Answers* by Roland Heifetz which reinforces the focus on leading through people.

He writes about the pressures that leaders face and their need to provide a "holding" space where others can act. This is especially true in times of change when the need for integrity is never higher.

Leaders need to be aware of the challenges and support people so that their level of distress isn't so high that they cannot act or lose confidence. Leaders also take responsibility rather than scapegoating and as soon as feasible give work back to the people.

Following on from this Thomas J Rice, *(Thriving in the Leadership Crucible: Who Does, Does Not and Why)* makes the point about authenticity even more strongly. The Leadership Crucible is that space within an organisation where all leaders find themselves sooner or later.

It is where there are genuine irreconcilable differences beyond different people and where the leader has to choose options that will cause grief to at least one group. Many leaders burn out because of all this pressure. Those who thrive are the Inner Leaders who have the character and self-knowledge to live according to a set of core values. They also are able to face up to hard truths and to relate to others.

These types of leaders and their organisations can be found especially in Servant-Leadership organisations which combine business success with high standards of people care. For example Southwest Airlines has made profits for more than 35 years. It also has the lowest number of complaints per passenger in the USA.

Southwest's mission statement reads as follows:

> *Southwest Airlines is dedicated to the highest quality of Customer Service delivered with a sense of warmth, friendliness, individual pride, and Company Spirit.*

Developing Inner Leadership

We are committed to provide our Employees a stable work environment with equal opportunity for learning and personal growth Creativity and innovation are encouraged for improving the effectiveness of Southwest Airlines Above all, Employees will be provided with the same concern, respect, and caring attitude within the Organisation that they are expected to share externally with every Southwest Customer.

There is also TDIndustries. TDIndustries was number two in the 100 best companies to work for in the USA in 1999 and has been consistently in the top ten. It has 1,500 employees. Its business is air-conditioning and plumbing. TDIndustries is explicit about its focus on applying the Servant Leadership model of Robert Greenleaf.

Its Mission Statement:

TDIndustries customers and employees work together in a partnership of the spirit to fulfill its mission. We are committed to providing **outstanding Career Opportunities** *by exceeding our Customers' Expectations through Continuous Aggressive Improvement.*

The critical point that comes from examining these Servant-Leadership companies is that it is possible to focus on people and be highly successful. In fact often the success has happened precisely because of that focus and the Inner Leader understands and acts on this.

So, as an Inner Leader, ask yourself: What are your own values and strengths? How best do you serve people in terms of your leadership? This may be in a number of ways related to the organisational functions that were discussed earlier. You may be best at getting new business for the organisation, at handling contracts, at producing high quality goods, at helping people. Each one of these ways of working can be seen as serving others.

Recognising your strengths and preferences is the first step. Understanding and recognising the different and diverse contributions of others is the second. It takes maturity and confidence to recognise that the different ways in which other people work is as valid as yours and even more so to encourage them in their own path.

Next, look at your organisation. What is its moral purpose? How does it serve others? Nigel Springett has done research in the UK on mission statements of different companies. Those which had a purpose that focused on delivering value to customers were more likely to have successful business results than those which focused on maximising returns to shareholders.

What are your organisation's values and purpose? Are these morally and ethically sound? Do they lead to congruent structures and processes that are true to these values? Are all areas and functions of the organisation equally honoured?

Exercise 31: Leading my Organisation,
    regardless of my position in it.

What and how do I contribute to the organisation and its purpose??

How do others contribute to the organisation and its purpose?

How does my organisation demonstrate its values?

What can I do to be more of a leader within my organisation?

The Gallup Organisation found in their research (*First Break all the Rules*) that even in badly run organisations there were pockets of superb performance and high motivation. This was a direct result of good individual leadership: a demonstration of Inner Leadership in action, making an enormous, positive difference in its immediate surroundings – even if the organisation overall was performing poorly.

One of the key ways to make organisations more people focused and efficient is by developing a "Yes-culture" organisation. Jaap Huttenga (*Servant-Leadership: Bringing the Spirit of Work to Work*) writes about the yes-culture of Hans Becker.

He is the CEO of the umbrella-organisation Humanitas which runs care homes for the elderly. They have 28 homes, 6,000 elderly people, and 2,300 personnel in the Netherlands. In his organisation the answer to every sincere question or proposal, whether it comes from residents or staff, is "Yes". Staff then have two weeks to try to achieve the "yes" result; sometimes of course they cannot, but at least they try.

It may seem that this is ridiculous and also extremely wasteful of money. However, Becker is one of the few managing directors in the care sector who has no financial problems. As he says, "A 'Yes-culture' is cheaper than a 'No-culture.'" The fundamental positive attitude towards personal needs and wishes creates a positive and affirming atmosphere.

One way in which to get to "yes" is to develop Amplifier meetings instead of Filter meetings. In Filter meetings people tend to block and point out why things won't work.

Rackham and Carlisle who researched this area in the UK, found that at least 70 per cent of meetings were Filter type meetings and only 4 per cent were Amplifier. The remaining 26 per cent were a mixture of the two types.

During Amplifier meetings people build on suggestions and focus on how ideas could work. Needless to say people at these meetings were far more committed to achieving the goals and the outcomes are actually better solutions and decisions. It is an error to think that we get better decisions by arguing and blocking – we don't!

Exercise 32: Developing a "Yes" Organisation

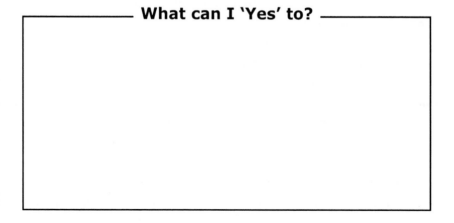

What can I 'Yes' to?

Where can I use amplifier and building behaviours?

C. Decisions, Decisions

What is a good company to work for? One that seeks to maximise the potential of every employee, that provides a creative, stimulating environment full of great ideas where everyone flourishes.

Michael Faust, *The Hermetic Disproof of M-Theory*

Decision-making and problem solving are key components of leadership. What the Inner Leader does is recognise that ultimately all choices and preferences come from values.

This is not to say that rational analysis should not be used but we need to guard against our biases. *Risk - the Science and Politics of Fear* by Dan Gardner is a superb analysis of the way bias and misguided thinking affect our judgement.

To give an example, newspapers in the USA quote that 50-70000 children are abducted every year and hence many parents live in fear of this happening to their children. There is no evidence at all for these figures; they are used to make sensational points. When the FBI figures are examined the true figure is only 115 children abducted annually year by strangers of whom 57% were returned unharmed within 24 hours. That still left 50 children harmed or killed which is appalling for those children and their families, but not the figures of tens of thousands that are quoted. In the same year 285 American children drowned in swimming pools yet there is no media attention or fear produced about this.

As Gardner says we are the healthiest, wealthiest generation in history, but the media and politics of fear stop us from enjoying this. Hence, we need to guard against the biases which stop us from being in touch with our own well-informed values, whether these biases come from others, as above, or our internal judgements.

The wise Inner Leader will study and work towards clear and appropriate critical thinking.

There are many ways of doing this; techniques such as force-field analysis and the fishbone technique (visual ways of presenting key factors that affect decisions), but all require checking with others to make certain that bias hasn't crept in and that decisions taken are well-grounded.

Linked to clear critical analysis is creativity. There are generally seen to be two forms of creativity. These have been defined as Adaptive and Innovative.

Adaptors are those who use their creativity to come up with multiple options and factors working within a given framework. For example, given a limited set of resources within a clear overall framework, how many potential ways of reaching a particular goal are there? The Adaptive form of creativity then comes into its own.

The Innovative form of creativity, on the other hand, consists of taking a radical look at the framework itself and modifying it. An example of this would be asking the question `What is employment?' and redefining employment as being engaged in any work activity, not just paid; in other words looking at and re-examining basic assumptions.

A useful alternative phrase for this process is 'reframing' – that is, changing the framework of our thoughts in the way we look at things.

Neither form of creativity is superior to the other but, again, individuals have a bias towards one or other of these forms

Exercise 33: Using Critical and Creativity Thinking effectively?

What skills do I need to improve to become wiser in making decisions?

What critical thinking and creativity skills and techniques am I good at?

What will I do to apply good decision making to my leadership issues?

Both critical thinking and creativity are needed to make the decisions which set the direction for the organisation. Again this requires analysing both the external world and the inner world of the organisation and the task/people dimensions.

We can use the Vital Questions from earlier and apply them to organisations as well.

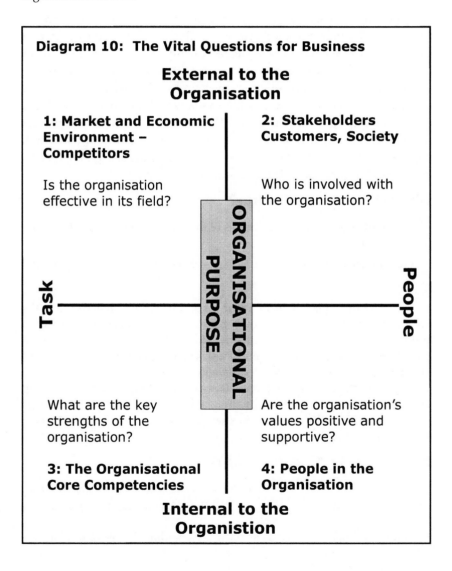

Diagram 10: The Vital Questions for Business

External to the Organisation

1: Market and Economic Environment – Competitors

Is the organisation effective in its field?

2: Stakeholders Customers, Society

Who is involved with the organisation?

Task

People

ORGANISATIONAL PURPOSE

What are the key strengths of the organisation?

Are the organisation's values positive and supportive?

3: The Organisational Core Competencies

4: People in the Organisation

Internal to the Organistion

Organisational Purpose

The starting point of course for any analysis must begin with the purpose of the organisation and what it contributes to others and to the world. How does your organisation add value and in what way and to whom?

What's the world like?

Quadrant 1: What's the marketplace and environment like? What are the trends? Who are the competitors? We need to think carefully about the concept of competitors. Standard usage suggests win-lose and a fight; but Inner Leadership thinking can change this to a win-win way of viewing them.

Quadrant 2: Who are your customers? And what are the "rules" and demands of the society you work within, its laws and ways of working? What can you do and what mustn't you do? The key here is that customers will get more powerful and will be able to dictate to companies what they want. Organisations need to relate and respond to these personal and idiosyncratic demands. (*The Intention Economy* by Searls)

What's the organisation like?

Quadrant 3: What are the strengths of the organisation? And is it making the most of these?

Quadrant 4: What are the organisation's values and even more importantly its identity or brand?

When all four quadrants are lined up and in sync with each other, the organisation is in a position to develop a strategy which is true to its values and its purpose, and which has integrity at its core: in essence, it becomes an Inner Leader organisation. Theoretically, this may appear straightforward, but in practice, of course, it can be very difficult to achieve.

A good start, perhaps, is to put in place a clear and robust decision-making process, based around the four quadrants; to monitor carefully that this is producing good results; and to make changes when necessary, without losing sight of the core values.

D. Owning the "Business" of You

> *If you're not in business for fun or profit – get out*
> **Robert Townsend,** *Up the Organisation*

You can think of yourself as a "business", not literally of course, but as a way of looking at your work and contribution to the world. It doesn't matter whether you work for a large corporation, the government, a charity or work at home as a parent; you can still feel as if you own your own business – that is you! By thinking in this way you can look at the services you offer to others, the rewards you get and your strengths and how you are able to use them.

So, given this way of thinking of yourself as a business why do you do what you do? Is it for fun, caring, or for profit? If it is for profit are you having fun? Profit and enjoyment don't always go together, but when they do it's a powerful combination with multiple rewards. What is unique about you? People who succeed in business understand that they have to do things in their own unique and magnificent way – not follow the "rules" laid down by others Therefore, imagining yourself as a business, how would that affect the vital questions you answered earlier on in this book?

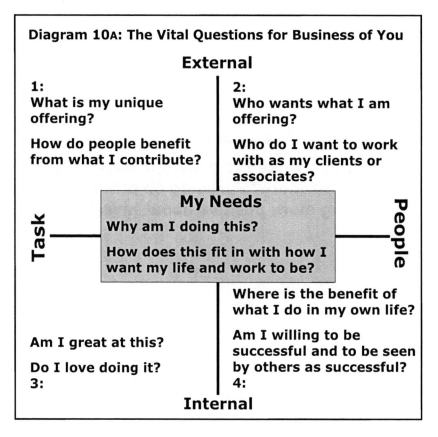

Diagram 10A: The Vital Questions for Business of You

External

1:
What is my unique offering?

How do people benefit from what I contribute?

2:
Who wants what I am offering?

Who do I want to work with as my clients or associates?

Task

My Needs

Why am I doing this?

How does this fit in with how I want my life and work to be?

People

Where is the benefit of what I do in my own life?

Am I great at this?

Do I love doing it?
3:

Am I willing to be successful and to be seen by others as successful?
4:

Internal

Allow yourself to be open to the possibilities that exist all around you and recognise the opportunities that are waiting for you; don't block these if they are not quite what you imagined. And welcome to the successful business of YOU.

Exercise 34: Owning the Business of You

What are my strengths as a "business"?
What is my unique contribution?
How do I add value to others?

Where do I need to develop? Marketing myself more? Focusing on others? Being more positive about myself?

Chapter 7

Inner Leadership and Play

A. Playfulness and Artistry

For to declare it once and for all, man plays only when he is in the full sense of the word a man, and he is only wholly man when he is playing.

Schiller quoted by Carl Jung

The few people I have known who were in the best contact with the deeper levels have been buoyant, fun-loving people with a light touch. The lady farmer who spoke about driving hard with a light hand was one of these. She not only had the gift; she knew what it was and could talk about it. Great as was her concern for the problems of the world and serious as was her intent in grappling with them, she had a light fun-loving approach to everything. Her house rang with laughter. It was a happy, healthy, constructive place.

Greenleaf

If work isn't fun and joyful and creative then it should be made so. One of the many self-limiting beliefs from the Shadow is that life is hard. Well yes and no...

We do have choices on whether to focus on half-full or half-empty glasses. And the energy and vibrancy of playfulness lightens everyone's world. Humour is often left out of lists of essential characteristics for leaders whereas it should be at the top. Inner Leaders don't take themselves too seriously and use their leadership to make life easier and more joyful for all.

One way to encourage play is by creativity and artistry. This could be any activity: it isn't just about painting or music or writing. Sport, for example, can give us all this and more; so can being in touch with nature.

The key is to feel in the "flow"; you love what you are doing so much then time disappears. Everyday activities can be made expressions of our creative talent. There is a lovely story of chambermaids in one hotel propping up children's teddy bears in front of the hotel room televisions and leaving notes for the children to find about what Teddy was doing; an example of creativity in the most mundane situation.

Some key points about artistry:

It is about caring and thoughtfulness with regard to what is being done. It is often a group process; working with others can be very rewarding and stimulating. By building on others' ideas we can get to unknown and exciting places.

Stressful and difficult areas in work or life can be sources of inspiration. Often we need to let our natural creativity just happen and not force it.

Structures and rules are needed. Although this may seem counter-intuitive, discipline can help creativity to emerge.

Creativity is everywhere, just waiting for us to recognise and engage with it. An inspiring introduction to discovering your inner artist is to read *The Artist's Way* by Julia Cameron. She suggests lots of brilliant things to do, including a weekly "Artist's Date".

Thomas Severin, in his book *Team, Leadership and Coaching*, suggests many ways of introducing art into coaching and leadership. For example, taking leaders to art galleries, asking them for interpretations of paintings in terms of their own values and those of their organisation; reading short stories and saying what that means about the culture of a country and many other exercises to unlock leaders' creativity.

For example the John Ford film *Stagecoach* although made in the 1930's offers much about the banking world today and the stereotypes we all have of each other. Art takes us away from the familiar and allows us to return with new insights and perspectives.

Exercise 35: Allowing Fun, Creativity and Play into Your Life

I am not a businessman, I am an artist
Warren Buffett

Can you make an Artist's date, a time for your own creativity, each week starting with…

Where can I add some fun, creativity and play in my daily routine?

How can I develop a sense of playfulness?

Where and how I can be an artist?

How can I create opportunities?

B. Abundance and Happiness – Saying Yes

We found that, as Aristotle argued 2,400 years ago, the more virtue-building activities people engaged in, the happier they said they were both on the day in question and on the following day. Perhaps surprisingly, there was no relationship between pleasure-seeking and happiness.

Michael Steger

Abundance and happiness are states of mind and heart. They are about seeing the glass always half full or even better totally full. The happiest, most successful people tend to be those who reminisce positively about the past, savour the present, and are optimistic about the future. This is not about false optimism or cheer but essentially appreciating what is and being grateful for the riches that it brings.

Inner Leaders can encourage this attitude in others and help them develop a virtuous circle – the more people focus on the positives the more they become happier and then they are more inclined to focus on the positives...

One specific way of doing this is for people to write down three things that went well every day for a week.

By also noting the causes of the positive events people can begin to see how they can increase their positive states of being. Research showed that this lifted happiness for a full six months, as did the "using signature strengths" method. In this exercise people take a test to identify their personal strengths, like creativity or forgiveness, and used a "top strength" in a new, different way daily for a week.

Research also shows that the things that make people happiest are sport, music and best of all – dancing.

Allied to this is "Wellness"; looking after our physical, emotional and mental needs. Eating, sleeping, drinking, exercising in ways that we enjoy and are supportive of who we are.

Abundance starts with appreciation and acceptance of who we are and where we are. This is about "Saying Yes" to all of the different parts of us including the so-called "bad" bits. Make no mistake: for many of us this can be a big deal.

Many of us have memories of school and families where criticism was the normal approach and it was regarded as arrogance to appreciate what you are. However, when we start from the positives and accept them fully then we can deal with the so-called imperfect parts of ourselves in a much better way.

Take an audit of your needs in each of these key areas and look at what you choose to do to be truly abundant and happy in each area and to say yes to them.

Exercise 36: Saying Yes

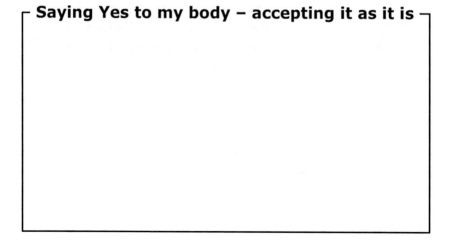

Saying Yes to my body – accepting it as it is

Saying Yes to my emotions

**Saying Yes to all of me, including my best
and my worst**

**Saying Yes to others: allowing them to be
as they are without complaining or trying
to change them**

Saying Yes to how I can and will be more creative and playful

```




```

Exercise 37: Poems for Yes

Find and read the following:
(or better still write or find your own!)

God Says Yes	Kaylin Haught
Yeah Yeah Yeah Song	The Flaming Lips
This be the Worst	Adrian Mitchell

Body

Wild Geese	Mary Oliver

Emotions

This being human	Rumi
You mustn't be frightened	Rainer Maria Rilke

All of You

Our fear is not that we are inadequate	Marianne Williamson
Love after Love	Derek Walcott
Give Yourself a Hug	Grace Nicholls

The Shadow

Gift of the Flaw	Antonio Machado
Anthem	Leonard Cohen

Others

Threads	Jim Autry

Creativity

It's Time	Jim Warda
Tripping over joy	Hafiz

The Future

Sometimes	Sheenagh Pugh
Ithika	C.P. Cavafy
The Summer Day	Mary Oliver
I will not die an unlived life	Dawna Markova

Anything by Rumi
(almost all of his poems relate to acceptance and saying yes to life).

C. Spirituality

> *To penetrate into the essence of all being and to*
> *release that fragrance of inner being for the guidance and benefit*
> *of others by expressing in the world of forms,*
> *truth, love, purity and beauty...*
> *this is the sole game which has intrinsic and absolute worth*
> **Meher Baba**

True Inner Leadership is a process of bringing yourself into the present moment and being in touch with your deepest drives and dreams.

When you are aligned with all levels of your being the truth of your spiritual intelligence will flow out into the world. Spirituality can be defined in many ways, but here it is about this being in connection with your Self. Self, as defined by Jung, is the sum total of all of who we are; fully complete and whole and above space and time.

Sometimes people refer to the Self as the Higher Self or the True Self. It doesn't matter what the terms are; the point is to connect and be guided by our noblest instincts. It is to be "whole". This is true spirituality.

One of the best ways to be in touch with our Self is intuition. Intuition is a great gift for us all. It is a way of seeing what could be and understanding things directly without the use of logical steps. It often only comes after years of practice and experience and can be an incredibly quick and useful way of making decisions. If intuition is directed towards the outer world then it's about opportunities and possibilities as developed by entrepreneurs for example. Inner directed intuition is more about personal growth.

The key problem with intuition is that our hopes and fears get in the way and distort the outcomes.

We need "true" intuition, to get rid of our biases and, by examining with honesty (perhaps with others) discover whether we are being authentic in our intuition. It is very easy to impose our subconscious wishes on the issue or decision. We have to give up that need to be in control and allow what will be to happen!

Exercise 38: Spirituality and me

┌─────── **Spiritual connection for me is like:** ───────┐
│   │
│   │
│   │
│   │
│   │
│   │
│   │
└──┘

I deepen my sense of connection and completeness by:

Chapter 8

The Selfdom Model

Introduction

The Selfdom Model or Framework is a way of bringing together all the work you have done in the sections on the Vital Questions, your story, being your best, companions, organisations and creativity.

It is a way of keeping all your insights together and also a method of focusing on further actions and continued individual growth.

At the centre of this is you as the Inner Leader – the ruler of your domain. You as an Inner Leader have to carry out many functions: dealing with people, organising work, analysis and decision-making and following your own unique path.

These functions can be seen as the many roles we have to play – and not just as an Inner Leader.

We all have roles as someone's daughter or son and many of us have roles as parents for example. For each of these roles we use different strengths and behave in different ways. Sometimes it can be difficult balancing all these roles and at times we get confused between them.

By using this framework you can clarify what it is you need to do in different roles and work on internal conflicts you may have. E.g. balancing personal needs with others' demands

The model is like that of a building which represents you and your personality. It is a well-used metaphor. For example Caroline Myss has written about St Teresa of Avila's use of the castle as an image for her spiritual journey. Whether you think of this as a castle or building or just an open space or diagram is not important.

What is important is that the Inner Leader is in the centre and the various roles in the Selfdom Model are allocated around the centre. Explanations of each of the titles and the roles they carry out follow later. You can work your way through these directly or, if you prefer, use the visualisation process suggested.

Selfdom Visualisation

Start by imagining you are out on a walk and it's one of those beautiful days that you love. You are enjoying every step you take. You can be by yourself or with someone close; a good friend, perhaps, or a partner. As you continue on your path you see ahead a magnificent building – a castle or some other structure. Despite the imposing size of the building, it seems warm and welcoming.

You approach and see a Gatekeeper who welcomes you. Describe him or her to yourself. They ask what you would like to do and you reply: "I wish to enter the castle" so you are welcomed in with a smile. You are very well aware that they could easily keep out anyone they do not want to let in.

As you enter the building you see that there is a plan to it (see below). There are four quarters divided North-South, East-West. And in each area there are two figures that carry out the functions needed to run different aspects of the building and the lives of the people in it.

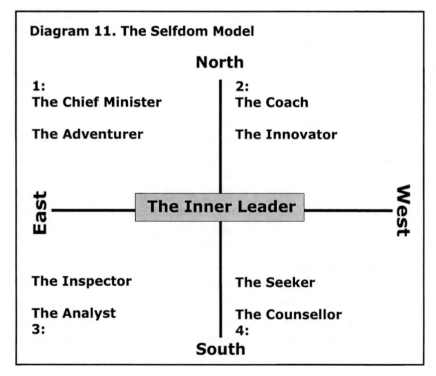

Diagram 11. The Selfdom Model

North

1:
The Chief Minister

The Adventurer

2:
The Coach

The Innovator

East ———— **The Inner Leader** ———— **West**

The Inspector

The Analyst
3:

The Seeker

The Counsellor
4:

South

At the centre of the building is the Inner Leader on his or her throne; wise and compassionate yet capable of being strong and forceful when necessary. You are naturally drawn to them as you recognise some of your own leadership characteristics in them. You are invited through to them and they ask you what it is you would like to have help with. When you have told them they smile wisely and sympathetically and suggest you visit one of the people who works for them and who can most help you.

You choose an appropriate person and go up to them and tell them your issue. You ask their advice and listen to their words and thank them. If there are other issues you repeat the process.

When you have finished your exploration you thank everyone and leave the building with a final thanks to the Gatekeeper and return back on the path until you reach the here and now.

Exercise 39: Developing Your Own Selfdom Model

This is something to be done slowly – over weeks, maybe months. Start with an area which is most urgent for you and stay with that. For that area complete the following:

Which person represents your ideal for that character?
E.g. The Chief Minister could be a statesman of some kind.
The person could be real, fictional or even dead.
It doesn't matter what they are as long as they are meaningful to you.

What qualities do they have?

What are your personal issues in that area?
E.g. The Coach could represent people issues

What advice would you via that character give yourself about that issue?

What actions will you take to get the outcome you want?

The Adventurer: Practical Skill and Adventure.

He or she is someone who wants to experience life to its full through being active and just doing it. Great at sports or willing to have a go, matter-of-fact and down to earth with a practical action-focused solution for any problems.

You would go to them when you just need to do try something new with an element of risk!

The Adventurer:
Person representing the character

Qualities:

_____

Personal issues:

_____

Desired outcomes:

_____

Advice:

_____

Actions:

_____

The Chief Minister: Dealing with the Practical World.

The Chief Minister is the organiser and driver for results. He or she makes certain that things happen according to schedules and plans. They are great at time management and keeping themselves and others organised and doing what needs to be done.

You would ask them for help in getting things done at a practical level... making it happen!

The Chief Minister:
Person representing the character

Qualities:

_____

Personal issues:

_____

Desired outcomes:

_____

Advice:

_____

Actions:

_____

The Coach: Dealing with People and Relationships.

This person has a concern for people and their values. They are focused on relationships and others' welfare. They can be equally tough and ready to challenge if they feel people are not being true to their words.

You would go to them for advice on intimate relationships, friends and working with colleagues – especially around the area of getting your voice heard.

The Coach:

Person representing the character

Qualities:

Personal issues:

Desired outcomes:

Advice:

Actions:

The Innovator: Possibilities and Play.

The Innovator likes experimenting with new ways and going where no one has gone before. He or she is quick, imaginative and always ready to see opportunities. They keep looking for what else is possible and they love change.

You would go to them for guidance on new possibilities and ways that you hadn't yet imagined.

The Innovator:
Person representing the character

Qualities:

Personal issues:

Desired outcomes:

Advice:

Actions:

The Seeker: Innermost Insights.

He or she is someone who is looking for meaning and insight often through their own inner world of imagination and intuition. They are most in tune with the mystical world that appears to be removed from the practical realities that most of us experience.

You would go to them for help in understanding your connection to that world and to get a sense of greater purpose in life.

The Seeker:
Person representing the character

Qualities:

Personal issues:

Desired outcomes:

Advice:

Actions:

The Counsellor: Dealing with Feelings.

He or she relies on their own subjective feelings and values to make sense of the world. They can be very empathetic as they understand how others are feeling. They also have a strong sense of integrity linked to their innermost values and represent your conscience.

You would go to them to check whether what you are doing is in tune with your deepest values and feelings. And also for help when dealing with the emotional distress of others.

The Counsellor:

Person representing the character

Qualities:

Personal issues:

Desired outcomes:

Advice:

Actions:

The Analyst: Analysis and In-depth Thinking.

The Analyst is logical and takes great delight in organising ideas and figures into patterns. This provides the ability to be objective and to see any flaws in plans or reasoning. They have great clarity of thought and think things through before acting hence their discipline of sticking to principles. Their advice in terms of planning and evaluating course of action is invaluable. They are also excellent at keeping track of finances.

When you need to weigh the pros and cons of a venture, idea or situation they will offer unbiased, solid advice. And can be invaluable in helping to keep your finances on an even keel.

The Inspector: Finishing Stuff and Keeping to High Standards.

He or she is a superb judge of life's experiences. They have a great eye for detail and are not happy unless things are finished according to the highest standards. This may be in the area of fine food or crafting a model. They have a superb ability to concentrate on specific details.

You would ask them for help when detailed focus is needed and things have to be just right.

The Inspector:

Person representing the character

Qualities:

Personal issues:

Desired outcomes:

Advice:

Actions:

The Inner Leader:

The Inner Leader is you. And for this you must develop your own approach as the unique and never-to-be-repeated individual you are. We are now full circle to the leader you most admired in Chapter 1 (Page 15).

You go to them for everything!

The Inner Leader:

Your ideal qualities

And the Key Messages from all this...

Diagram 12. Key Selfdom Messages

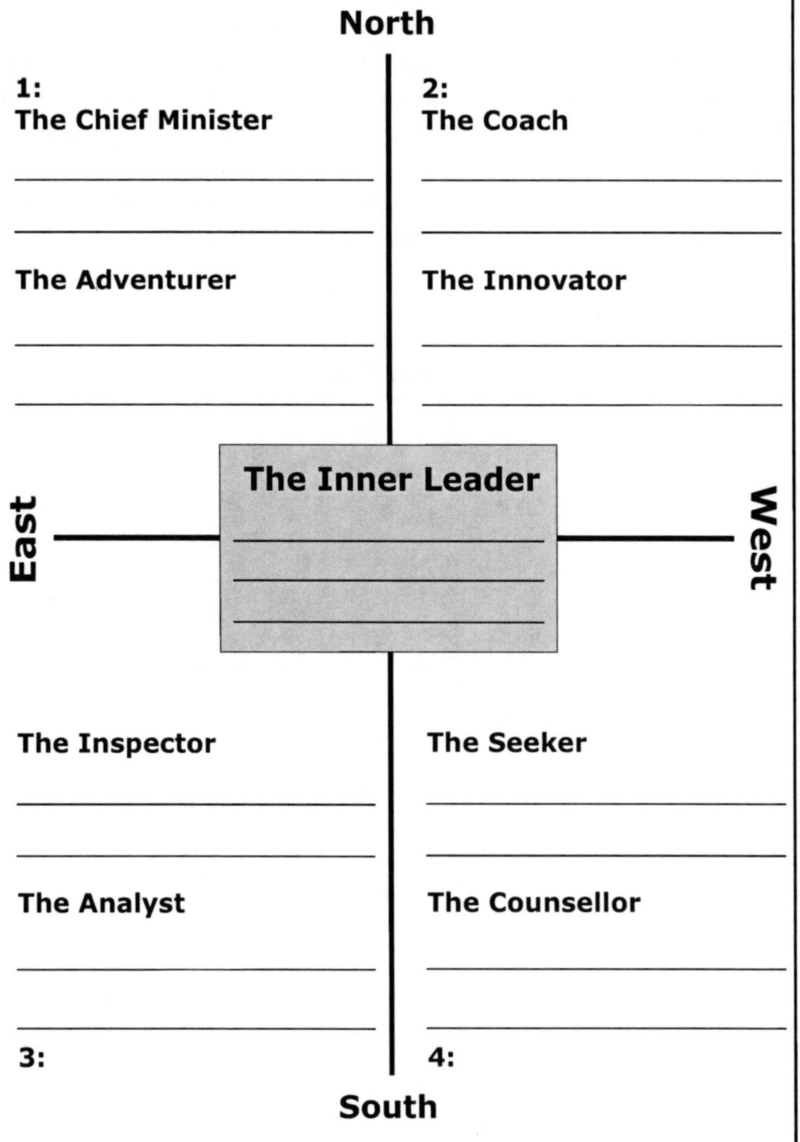

North

1:
The Chief Minister

_____

_____

The Adventurer

_____

_____

2:
The Coach

_____

_____

The Innovator

_____

_____

East

The Inner Leader

_____

_____

_____

West

The Inspector

_____

_____

The Analyst

_____

_____

3:

The Seeker

_____

_____

The Counsellor

_____

_____

4:

South

And in the End

The love you take is equal to the love you make…..

School is over – it has been for a long time. There are no more head teachers and exams except in your head. You, as an Inner Leader, are your own teacher and guide. Not that you cannot learn from others – that is essential as an Inner Leader, but you take what you need instead of accepting what is conventional wisdom.

The clearer you become about you and your gifts and why the world needs you as you are then the more you will be a true Inner Leader.

Have fun!

Chapter 8

Resources

There are a number of PDFs on my website – www.ralphlewis.co.uk – which can be downloaded to help with various sections. These are marked with an asterisk.

1. Introduction

Developmental Coaching – Working with the Self
    Tatiana Bachkirova, March 2011
Inner Work
    Robert Johnson, January 1991

2. Inner Leadership

Love and Profit
    James Autry, 1991
The Servant as Leader
    Robert Greenleaf
Servant-Leadership: Bringing the Spirit of Work to Work
    Ralph Lewis and John Noble, Management Books, 2000
Servant-Leadership
    www.greenleaf.org.uk
Management Development Beyond the Fringe
    Phil Lowe and Ralph Lewis, Kogan Page, 1994
The One Thing You Need to Know... about Great Managing, Great Leading and Sustained Individual Success
    Marcus Buckingham, October 2006
Finding Your Soul's Purpose
    www.centerforconsciousascension.net, Nicolas David Ngan
Busting Loose from the Business Game
    Robert Scheinfeld, July 2009
Inner Leadership
    Simon Smith, April 2000
One Piece of Paper: The Simple Approach to Powerful, Personal Leadership
    Mike Figiuolo, November 2011

The Inner-Work of Leadership
   Barry Brownstein, March 2010
Transitions, Making Sense of Life's Changes
   W Bridges, 1980
Beyond the Peter Principle*
   Ralph Lewis

3. Telling Your Story

Who would you be without your story?
   www.thework.com, Bryon Katie
The Seven Basic Plots – Why we tell stories
   Christopher Booker, November 2005
Crossing the Unknown Sea – Work as a Pilgrimage of Identity
   David Whyte, Riverhead Books, 2001
The Return of King Arthur – Completing the Quest for Wholeness, Inner Strength and Self-Knowledge
   Diana Durham, February 2005
The Grail Castle
   Kenneth Johnson and Marguerite Elsbeth, 1995
Passages – Predictable Crisis of Adult Life
   Gail Sheehy, January 1997
The Hero with a Thousand Faces
   Joseph Campbell, April 2012
The Power of Myth DVD
   Joseph Campbell with Bill Moyers
Your Best Year Yet
   Jinny Ditzler, January 2006
Money and Soul
   Per Espen Stoknes, August 2010
Time to Think: Listening to Ignite the Human Mind
   Nancy Kline, December 1998
Games People Play
   Eric Berne, January 2010
The Corporate Savage
   Martin Page, 1972

Credibility
James Kouzes and Barry Posner Josey-Bass 1993

4. Becoming Your Best

Bragging
www.bragbetter.com

Myers-Briggs and Servant-Leadership*
Ralph Lewis

Getting Things Done
David Allen, 2001

Now, Discover Your Strengths
Marcus Buckingham & Donald Clifton, 2001

Bounce
Matthew Syed, April 2011

Outliers
Malcolm Gladwell, June 2009

The Dark Side of the Light Chasers
Debbie Ford, August 2001

Inner Gold
Robert Johnson, June 2010

Practically Shameless
Alyce Barry, February 2008

Stress Management*
Ralph Lewis

Matrix Reimprinting
Karl Dawson and Sasha Allenby, August 2010

Happiness is Free
Hale Dwoskin, March 2011

Rational Recovery
Jack Trimpey, November 1996

Emotional Equations
Chip Conley, May 2012

Please Understand Me
Bates and Keirsey, May 1998

*Stress Management**
  Ralph Lewis
After Virtue
  Alistair Macintyre, 2007
*Developing a Leadership Practice**
  Ralph Lewis
Make Yourself Better
  Philip Weeks, 2012

5. Companions

People Skills
  R. Bolton, June 1986
Getting to Yes
  W Fisher and R Ury, 1997
Lying with the Heavenly Woman
  Robert Johnson, July 2009
*Confident Communication**
  Ralph Lewis
Presence: How to Use Positive Energy for Success in Every Situation
  Patsy Rodenburg, May 2009
Million Dollar Networking
  Andrea Nierenberg, September 2005
Life-Changing Conversations
  Sarah Rozenthuler, March 2012
The Social Animal
  David Brooks, January 2012

6. Leading in Organisations

Reading the Mind of the Organisation
  Annamaria Garden Gower, 2000
First, Break All the Rules
  Marcus Buckingham & Curt Coffman, 1999
True North: Discover Your Authentic Leadership
  David Gergen, Bill George and Peter Sims, April 2007
From Good to Great
  Jim Collins, October 2001

The impact of corporate purpose on strategy, organisations and financial performance
Nigel Springett

Creating the Good Life
James O'Toole, November 2005

The Happy Manifesto
Henry Stewart, November 2011

Employees First, Customers Second
Vineet Nayar, May 2010

The Power of Nice
Linda Kaplan and Robin Koval, April 2011

The Joy of Business
Simone Melasas, June 2012

The Business of Kindness
Olivia McIvor, January 2007

Leadership Without Easy Answers
Ronald Heifetz, 1994

The Intention Economy
Doc Searls, May 2012

Thinking, Fast and Slow
Daniel Kahneman, 2012

Risk: The Science and Politics of Fear
Dan Gardner, January 2009

Reading the Mind of the Organisation Review*
Ralph Lewis

From Chaos to Complexity*
Ralph Lewis

How can business people take wiser decisions?
www.peterowen.co.uk, Peter Owen 2012

Up the Organisation
Robert Townsend, 1977

Strategy and Organisational Development*
Ralph Lewis

Business Energetics
www.healthyinmind.com, Sejual Shah

7. Inner Leadership and Play

The Artist's Way,
Julia Cameron

Art to Inspire,
Ahrabella Heabe Lewis, www.ahrabellaheabelewis.co.uk

8. The Selfdom Model

Adventures in Healing
George SanFacon, 2011

Entering the Castle – An Inner Path to God and Your Soul
Caroline Myss, 2007

Internal Family Systems Therapy
www.selfleadership.org

Lightning Source UK Ltd.
Milton Keynes UK
UKOW05f0653080614

233041UK00001B/9/P